FIPS 140 Demystified

An Introductory Guide for Developers

FIPS 140 Demystified

An Introductory Guide for Developers

Wesley Hisao Higaki
Ray Potter

FIPS 140 Demystified: An Introductory Guide for Developers

ISBN-13: 978-1460990391

ISBN-10: 1460990390

Acknowledgments

We would like to thank all of the product developers who have gone through the FIPS 140 cryptographic module validation process with us. These projects helped to give us the breadth of experience and insights to write this book.

Special thanks go to Yukie Higaki for her work to design the book cover and to Naomi Higaki for her tireless editing.

About the Cover

To the uninitiated, the path through the FIPS 140 validation process is as obscure as walking through the mist across the Golden Gate Bridge on a typical San Francisco day. There are many unknowns and many questions that need to be answered. What are the requirements? What is the process? Who needs to be involved? What has to be done? Where do I start? *FIPS 140 Demystified: An Introductory Guide for Developers* was written to answer these questions.

Demystifying like de-mist-ifying or removing the fog so you can see where you are going is the subject of this book. The book's front cover shows how the fog across the Golden Gate obscures the path to the other side. The back cover shows the clear view of the Golden Gate and the way across it. *FIPS 140 Demystified: An Introductory Guide for Developers* helps lift the fog that lingers over the FIPS 140 cryptographic module validation standards and process so that the developer can see the path to success.

About the Authors

Wesley Hisao Higaki

Wes Higaki is the Director of Certifications Strategy at Apex Assurance Group. Wes authored and published *Successful Common Criteria Evaluations: A Practical Guide for Vendors* in 2010. Wes was the director of Software Assurance and Product Certifications at Symantec Corporation. He led all of the company's Common Criteria, FIPS-140 certifications, and ICSA Labs testing efforts. Wes served as a company spokesman addressing software assurance issues and has been an invited speaker at several conferences. He led several industry working groups dealing with product security certifications.

Wes co-founded and chaired the Common Criteria Vendors' Forum (CCVF), an organization of commercial product vendor company representatives gathered to discuss Common Criteria and CC-related issues, develop solutions, and drive action to improve the standards and policies around it.

Wes received a Bachelor of Science degree in mathematics from the University of California, Davis. He also has a Master of Science degree in computer science from Santa Clara University and serves on their industry advisory board.

About the Authors

Ray Potter

Ray Potter is the Managing Director of Apex Assurance Group and is responsible for the operations and delivery of the firm's consulting and program management services. Ray was formerly the manager of the Security Assurance Program at Cisco Systems, where he was responsible for the direction, strategy, and operations of Cisco's global security certification and assurance initiatives, including the FIPS 140, Common Criteria, and ICSA programs. He was the single point of contact for standards bodies, Cisco's customers, and Cisco's product teams.

Prior to working at Cisco Systems, Ray was a consultant with a global management consulting firm, assisting Fortune 500 companies and government agencies implement IT solutions and process improvement initiatives.

Ray has been published in *Information Security Magazine* and is a frequent guest speaker in industry forums and conferences on the subject of Information Assurance, risk management, and FIPS 140/Common Criteria.

About Apex Assurance Group

Apex Assurance Group was founded to provide Information Assurance consulting services with unrivalled attention to quality and customer service. Our mission is to help companies create opportunity, sustain competitive advantage, and increase market share in the Global Government space and the Information Assurance space.

Apex Assurance Group offers Security Certification Consulting services tailored to help customers to efficiently achieve third-party security certifications. Specific services for FIPS 140 and Common Criteria include the following:

- Product design assistance
- Education and training
- Project management for the entire validation process
- FIPS 140 Security Policy, Vendor Evidence, and Finite State Machine development
- FIPS 140 algorithm testing support
- Common Criteria Security Target development
- Common Criteria supporting evidence development

The firm's unique Security Assurance Strategy services help companies build a security assurance program and achieve organizational effectiveness, leading to a reduction in cost and time-to-market. Security Assurance Strategy services include the following components:

- Lifecycle Program Management
- Certifications Strategy
- Education and Training
- Communications Strategy
- Software Development

Table of Contents

Table of Figures

Table of Tables

PART 1: BACKGROUND

In this part:

Chapter 1: Introduction

Since the times of Julius Caesar, cryptography has been used to hide secrets from unauthorized persons. The Caesar cipher was used by the ancient Roman warriors to encode messages during battle. While this cipher is an old and primitive ancestor to modern cryptographic algorithms, the purpose was the same as today – protect data from prying eyes. The struggle to protect confidential information continued through World War II when the German Enigma machine became famous for encrypting messages so successfully. Cracking the Enigma machines' codes brought about the formation of organizations such as the U.S. National Security Agency assembling expert analysts and mathematicians bent on developing technological advances in cryptography.

Today, common citizens around the world use cryptography in everyday life. Billions of dollars per day of online credit card transactions are protected using some form of data encryption. Businesses use encrypted email to protect confidential, competitive information. Corporate and private laptop users encrypt their hard drives in order to protect their data in case the computer is lost or stolen. We, like the Romans, rely on encryption to protect data from unauthorized access.

Cryptography has evolved into a sophisticated science requiring the greatest mathematicians and computer scientists to develop new and improved cryptographic algorithms. As computing power increases and attackers hone their capabilities over time, older algorithms show signs of weakness. The once-vaunted Data Encryption Standard (DES) algorithm is now considered insecure against today's attacks. Its relatively small 56-bit key length makes it vulnerable to brute force attacks with modern computers. The Advanced Encryption Standard (AES) has replaced DES as an accepted, secure algorithm.

It is not enough to merely have developed an encryption algorithm and to mathematically prove that it is secure against modern attacks. Using approved, standardized methods these implementations must be proven to have correctly implemented these algorithms. The U.S. National Institute of Standards and Technology (NIST) created the Cryptographic Module Validation Program (CMVP) to provide the infrastructure to validate that cryptographic modules used approved algorithms and have implemented them properly. NIST created the Federal Information Processing Standard 140 (FIPS 140) to document the standard cryptographic validation requirements.

Consumers using these validated modules can be confident that their data is encrypted using proven techniques and that any security claims have been validated by an accredited, independent third-party testing laboratory.

Many product developers want to provide their customers with the highest level of assurance possible, so they choose to submit their products to the FIPS 140 validation process. Some developers may start this process by reading the complex NIST documentation and may become frustrated by the idiosyncrasies of the standards. Only the foolhardy "jump in without looking." The smart developers enlist the help of experts, but may not know where to start.

Developers have many questions initially and oftentimes do not know where to turn for sound, reasoned and business-savvy answers. They want to know how long it will take so that they can do effective resource allocation planning. They want to know how much money it will cost so that they can budget for these expenses. They need to know how to prepare their products so that they meet the feature requirements of FIPS 140. Expert consultants may have the answers to these questions, but can they be trusted to look out for the developers' best interests?

Motivation for this Book

As with many government-sponsored programs, the path toward successful completion of a FIPS 140 validation can be confusing, daunting and frustrating. Without expert guidance, the process can be expensive, both in terms of money spent and in time invested. Wasted time and money equate to diminished competitiveness and squandered opportunities. Many product developers that are faced with their first FIPS 140 validation effort will not know where to start. Even if they hire experts, they have little basis for trusting their guidance.

Due diligence is a business imperative when seeking the counsel of outside consultants. Checking references, searching the Internet and extensively interviewing candidates are all important steps in the due diligence process. What is oftentimes difficult to determine is how well the expert will serve as an agent or advocate for the product developer.

The purpose of this book is to provide product developers with some basic information so that they can be better prepared to navigate through the process more easily and more confidently. The information contained in this book will enable product developers to ask prospective consultants intelligent, insightful questions so that they can be assured that the advice they will receive will guide them toward an efficient, successful FIPS 140 cryptographic module validation.

The primary audience for this book is product developers who are faced with having to undergo their first FIPS 140 validation by sharing experiences to help the reader avoid the pitfalls that might lead to an expensive, unsuccessful validation. More experienced product developers also may benefit from the lessons learned and best practices through the experiences demonstrated in this book.

How this Book Is Organized

Part 1: Background gives the reader some essential background information in four chapters.

- Chapter 1: Introduction gives an overview of this book.
- Chapter 2: Threats and Risks describes today's threats to data security.
- Chapter 3: Encryption Is the Solution illustrates how cryptographic technologies address today's threats.
- Chapter 4: Basic Applied Cryptography gives a brief explanation for cryptographic technologies applicable to FIPS 140.

Part 2: FIPS 140 Overview contains four chapters on the technical details of the FIPS 140 standards and the overall validation process.

- Chapter 5: Algorithm Validation describes the Cryptographic Algorithm Validation Program (CAVP) and the algorithms recognized by FIPS 140.
- Chapter 6: Module Validation provides an overview of the Cryptographic Module Validation Program (CMVP) philosophy and history.
- Chapter 7: Costs and Timelines explains the investments and anticipated schedules of the FIPS 140 process.
- Chapter 8: Security Requirements reviews the FIPS 140 standards and the details of the Derived Test Requirements (DTR).

Part 3: Real-World Examples includes chapters highlighting situations and considerations for different product types based on real-world experiences.

- Chapter 9: Hardware Appliance illustrates some topics unique to FIPS 140 validations of appliance products.
- Chapter 10: Security Software Application describes concerns encountered during application software validations.
- Chapter 11: Data Encryption Library covers topics specific to software libraries.
- Chapter 12: USB Flash Drive explains issues encountered by single-chip cryptographic solutions.
- Chapter 13: Open Source Library reviews the trials and tribulations of the OpenSSL library FIPS 140 validations.

Part 4: Conclusions closes the book with a discussion on best practices for product developers, issues with FIPS 140, and the possible future of FIPS 140.

- Chapter 14: Best Practices reviews some practices that will ensure a successful cryptographic module validation.
- Chapter 15: Issues With FIPS 140 highlights the issues and weaknesses in the FIPS 140 validation process.
- Chapter 16: Future of FIPS 140 discusses some possible future paths and directions for the validation program.
- Chapter 17: Wrap-Up summarizes the book.

For the purposes of discussion in this book, the following definitions will be used. Cryptography (or cryptology) is defined as the practice and study of hiding information. Encryption (or encoding) is the process of transforming information into a form that is understandable only to those for which the information is intended. Cryptographic or encryption technology is the embodiment of the encryption process as in the form of hardware or software. A cryptographic module is a product or part of a product that encapsulates some cryptographic technology.

This book is based on FIPS 140-2 as of October 2010. At the time of this writing, FIPS 140-3 is still in draft form and the updated supporting documents (such as the Derived Test Requirements and Implementation Guidance) are not yet available. Chapter 16 discusses the differences between FIPS 140-2 and FIPS 140-3 based on the information available at the time of this writing.

Chapter 2: Threats and Risks

During wartime, encryption technologies have been used to protect military intelligence information from falling into the enemy's hands. The Germans in World War II used the famous Enigma machine to gain an advantage over Allied Forces. The threats they faced were matters of life and death – to conquer or be conquered. Encryption technology is still used in wartime to protect national intelligence information. The threats and risks are very high in war and the need to protect information is critical. However, encryption technology has found its way into nearly every facet of daily life for many people in the twenty-first century because of the broad availability of cryptographic technology and the need for information protection in this hyper-connected world.

Business enterprises rely more and more on information technology and e-commerce capabilities to conduct their business operations. Business-to-business (B2B) operations such as inventory control and supply chain management are now commonly performed using computers, software and the Internet. The need to protect the information flowing across these systems and across the Internet has grown with the increased network traffic and with the sophistication of the attackers. Financial information such as bank account and credit card numbers are routinely transferred between businesses and are an attractive target for Internet thieves. Corporate spies seek to learn more about their competitors' plans and intellectual property by sniffing networks or breaking into servers. All of this kind of corporate data needs strong protection and the companies need confidence that the protections they put in place are effective.

Consumers face similar threats as businesses when they interact with businesses and with other individuals online. Identity theft is a large and growing problem as credit card and other personally identifiable information (PII) is exposed to unauthorized parties. PII can be stolen or lost and then abused by those who seek to profit from these breaches. Repairing the damage done by identity theft not only costs money, it takes time, sometimes months, to repair.

The Lost Laptop Computer

In 2006, a U.S. Internal Revenue Service (IRS) employee lost a laptop computer containing thousands of IRS employee electronic fingerprint records. These fingerprint records were used for electronic access cards into IRS facilities. When this laptop was misplaced, there was a risk that someone would fabricate false identification access cards allowing unauthorized persons to enter IRS facilities. At the least, this incident represents an embarrassing situation for the IRS, a government agency charged with handling billions of U.S. citizens' tax dollars. In the worst case scenario, this breach could have enabled malicious parties to gain access to more confidential information such as the social security numbers, addresses, birth dates, and phone numbers of all U.S. taxpayers.

In another government laptop incident in 2006, a U.S. Veterans Administration employee's laptop was stolen during a home burglary. This laptop allegedly contained the social security numbers of 26 million veterans. What made this incident especially embarrassing is that it occurred just months after the IRS incident.

The U.S. National Institute of Health (NIH) lost a laptop in 2008 that contained 2,500 patients' cardiac study data. While this cardiac data may not outwardly appear to be particularly useful to anyone but the physicians treating these patients nor particularly harmful to the patients if the data is leaked, 7% of all identify theft is medical identity theft. Nonetheless, the loss of data represents a breach in security and illustrates the fragility of the safeguards we employ to protect private information.

Social security numbers are one of the key elements of establishing a financial identity in the United States. When someone applies for a credit card, they are typically asked for their name, address, phone number, mother's maiden name, and social security number. The assumption is that with this information the applicant is claiming they are who they say they are without repudiation. If the confidentiality of this personally identifiable information (PII) is compromised, unauthorized persons could assume another's identity. This is called identity theft.

Identity theft is on the rise. There were a reported 10 million cases of identity theft in the United States in 2009, up an estimated 10% from the year before. The costs of identity theft are great. It can take up to 2 years to clean up identity fraud with most cases taking up to one year. The average victim will spend over 300 hours recovering from identity theft. Businesses lose over 220 billion dollars a year to identity fraud [Javelin 2009]. Identity theft threats are real and the risks are high for everyday citizens.

Unsecured Internet Transactions

Commercial businesses from small restaurants to large, multi-national corporations rely on the Internet to transact their business-to-customer (B2C) as well as their business-to-business (B2B) electronic interactions. Even small businesses will handle several hundred thousand dollars in customer receipts as well as several more hundreds of thousands of dollars in transactions with suppliers in one year. Many of these transactions will be handled electronically. Many customers will pay by credit or debit card. These transactions will be handled using electronic card readers connected to automated payment systems. Suppliers will send invoices electronically to the corporate accounts payable staff and payments will be made automatically through the firm's computerized systems. Businesses of all sizes around the world depend heavily on the Internet.

In 2008, e-commerce accounted for 3.7 trillion dollars in U.S. sales, shipments and revenues [EStats 2010]. This was an increase of 12% over the previous year. Individual consumers tend to think of e-commerce as online transactions that they typically deal with such as: banking (transfers and bill paying), securities trading, and purchases. However, the bulk of U.S. online transactions (over 92%) in 2008 were business-to-business (B2B) transactions. These statistics illustrate that not only should consumers be concerned for the security of their online transactions, but businesses have a lot at stake as well.

Consumers are concerned with identity theft. Businesses relying on the Internet need to be concerned with ensuring that all of their financial transactions are being performed accurately, correctly and in a timely manner. They need to be sure that the financial data they are transmitting and storing is secure. Disruption in the flow of this information can result in lost business. Unauthorized leakage of this information may lead to fines or lawsuits.

The Payment Card Industry has established a Data Security Standard (PCI-DSS) to protect the transmission, processing and storage of payment card data including cardholder data. Unlike many other data security standards, the PCI-DSS is an industry-led effort to ensure that vendors (including small establishments) follow reasonable measures to ensure the security of their online transactions. The payment card industry felt it necessary to establish these standards because of the growing threat of data breaches and the impact these breaches would have on the reputation of the entire payment card industry and e-commerce.

Unsecured Email Messages

Secret messages are the hallmark of spy novels. Important messages are transmitted to field agents. These messages are encrypted (encoded) so that only the intended recipient can decode the message with the secret key that the agent was given prior to accepting the assignment. Strong (i.e. complex) encryption algorithms are used to encode the message to ensure that the message cannot be read or modified by unauthorized parties. In spy novels the success of the mission depends on the true contents of the message being securely delivered to the agent.

While most messages that consumers and businesses send and receive every day are a lot less dramatic than the secret agent's, they do sometimes convey sensitive information that should not be shared beyond the intended audience. Businesses exchange quotes and invoices. Individuals share personal and private information. These days, these messages are sent quite frequently via electronic mail or some other electronic messaging system such as instant messaging and text messaging.

Suppliers in stiff competition for multi-million dollar projects need to be sure that the email messages with their project proposals and pricing quote do not fall into the wrong hands. Unscrupulous competitors could use such information to provide a winning bid.

Summary

The threats of disclosing confidential information are real and growing with the ubiquity of the Internet in everyday lives. The risks of loss and damage also grow as the dependence on the Internet grows. Protecting confidential electronic information has now become a critical issue for consumers and businesses around the world – it is no longer just for spies and warriors; it is an issue for everyone.

Chapter 3: Encryption Is the Solution

The previous chapter highlighted the threats and risks to electronic information in today's highly-connected world. There are many computer and network security technologies available to consumers and enterprises including firewalls, anti-virus software, and intrusion detection systems. While all of these protection technologies serve their purpose, encryption is the foundational technology used to protect data. Encryption is the last line of defense.

The Caesar Cipher

A cipher is a simple character substitution encoding scheme. A letter in the alphabet is replaced by another letter in the encoded message. Like the secret decoder ring that was popular in breakfast cereal boxes of the 1960's, the trick to decoding the messages was to know the shift in the alphabet that was used to encode the message.

For example, if the word "chip" were to be encoded using a three-letter offset cipher, the "c" in "chip" would appear as an "f" in the encoded message since "f" is three letters away from "c" in the alphabet. The "h" would be replaced by a "k"; the "i" with an "l"; and "p" would be represented by an "s". The word "chip" would be encoded using the three-letter offset as "fkls".

To illustrate the cipher, the English alphabet is lined up at the top of the diagram below. The three-letter shift cipher is shown below the alphabet. To code any word or message using this scheme the sender merely replaces the letter from the top row with the letter from the bottom row.

Julius Caesar used the cipher to encode messages to his troops during battle. This simple but clever mechanism allowed him to communicate securely in a hostile environment where secrecy was paramount.

Encryption technologies have evolved in sophistication from the Caesar cipher which merely shifted character order in the alphabet to 256-bit symmetric keys used in today's Advanced Encryption Standard (AES). Encryption has always been a key data protection technology and has evolved with our security needs.

It is estimated that the worldwide market for electronic information security software technologies in 2010 will be over 16.5 billion dollars [Gartner 2010]. These revenue figures include products such as firewalls, virtual private networks, intrusion detection systems and anti-virus. While these products protect data and information systems in different ways, they merely provide the "outer layers" of protection in the "defense in depth" schemes commonly used today. Encryption protects the data when the other defense mechanisms fail. When a hacker wriggles through an open port in a firewall and gains root access to a server, the intrusion detection system may report the intrusion but cannot actively protect the data. In ancient times a Roman messenger may have been captured while trying to relay a message from Caesar but the cipher made the message unreadable. Similarly, modern electronic data encryption renders the bits on the disk useless to the hacker even after he has broken through all of the other barriers.

E-commerce has permeated all facets of consumer and business life to the point that protecting data is critical to not only the continued success of commerce but to its very survival. If consumers and businesses lose confidence in the security of their online transactions, e-commerce will cease. With so much at stake it is imperative that key security technologies such as cryptography keep ahead of the threats and attacks and continue to instill customer confidence.

Encrypting Data in Transit

Electronic data is most vulnerable when it is being transmitted across open, public networks. A clear example of this vulnerability is "war driving" which is when attackers, intruders and pirates gain unauthorized access to unsecured wireless networks by merely driving by wireless access points using some fairly unsophisticated equipment. Gaining network access is just the first step toward collecting confidential data. Data transmitted over these wireless networks could be "sniffed" and exploited by malicious parties.

Installing a set of wireless access points in an office building can save thousands of dollars in network installation costs compared to running miles of the traditional Category 6 Ethernet cable through the facility. Unfortunately, installers may not be thorough and can fail to enable the secure communications features on the access point devices. When the access points are activated, everyone (including unauthorized parties) may be able to connect to the network and view the data flow.

Confidential corporate email messages, files containing competitive information and other company private information flow across wireless network during any company's normal operation. Intellectual property, competitive information, and company secrets can be exposed to anyone with a wireless-enabled laptop that is parked outside the building. This problem can easily be solved by enabling the security features on the wireless access points. These security features encrypt the network traffic so that only authorized parties can read the data.

Encrypting Data at Rest

Data is also at risk when it is stored on media that is not in a completely controlled environment. Stolen and lost laptop computers plagued and embarrassed the IRS and NIH in 2006. Laptops can contain sensitive and confidential data. Laptops are portable and are easily transported from a secure environment such as the IRS offices to an unsecure environment such as the employees' favorite local lunchtime hang-out. The risks are high when the laptop contains thousands of social security numbers or trade secrets and the laptop is left behind on a chair at the restaurant.

Perhaps an even more ubiquitous and portable form of data storage is the USB flash drive. These lipstick-sized devices can carry gigabytes of valuable information. They are extremely convenient because they can be plugged into virtually any computer and used instantly making them a popular storage device. Because of their popularity and their small size, it is easy to see how these data storage devices could be misplaced or stolen. Since they are so convenient and ubiquitous, it is also easy to imagine that these little devices may contain lots of confidential information.

In November 2008, the U.S. Department of Defense (DOD) banned the use of USB storage devices after a device, infected with a worm affected many parts of the DOD networks. The ban lasted 15 months until the DOD decided that the USB devices were so pervasive that they had to continue their use. USB drives made it easy for DOD personnel to transfer large amounts of data to remote sites where network bandwidth was severely limited (e.g., ships at sea).

Sensitive, confidential data being transmitted or transported outside of secured, controlled environments are vulnerable to accidental or malicious exposure. Encrypting the data in transit and at rest prevents the data from being read or modified by unauthorized entities. Encryption is the last line of defense when the laptop containing trade secrets is lost or when electronic files are intercepted while being transferred across the Internet.

Customer Demand for Encryption

Today, many employees are able to work remotely from home offices or while travelling hundreds or thousands of miles away from their corporate email, file and web servers. These employees rely heavily on the virtual private network (VPN) software that enables secure communications between the remote location and the corporate servers. The VPN enable employees to connect to company compute resources as securely as if the client computer were hard-wired into the RJ-11 jacks in the corporate offices. The VPN encrypts the network traffic from the employee's computer to the company servers so that no one can decipher the messages and transactions that are being transferred.

Customers today also routinely use encryption technologies. Customer placing online orders enter their name, address, phone number, and credit card information into their "shopping cart" web page and press the "submit" button. The customer probably barely notices that the universal resource locator (URL) used for that web page starts with "https" rather than the more common "http". Hypertext Transport Protocol (HTTP) is the network protocol that enables web browsers such as Microsoft's Internet Explorer or Mozilla's Firefox to interact with application software running on remote servers. Information transferred between the user's client computer and the web servers use the international HTTP standard. To secure the transfer of confidential data such as credit card numbers, the Hypertext Transfer Protocol - Secure (HTTPS) is used. HTTPS combines HTTP with Secure Socket Layer/Transport Layer Security (SSL/TLS) cryptographic protocols to encrypt the communications between the web browsers and the web servers. With HTTPS, customers can be assured that credit card and other sensitive information cannot be stolen by a maleficent since the encrypted data will be unintelligible except to those with the proper authorization.

Use of encryption technologies such as VPN and HTTPS is commonplace by consumers and businesses everywhere. E-commerce has become the backbone of business transactions in the 21st century and encryption enables these transactions to occur securely and reliably.

Good business practice dictates the use of encryption to protect sensitive and confidential data. However, due to the publicity around some extensive data breaches, there has been an outcry for greater government oversight and regulation to allay the public's concerns. Identity theft and privacy concerns have caused legislators to enact regulations to protect consumer data, and in the event of an accidental or malicious breach, that affected citizens are notified.

Identity theft protection concerns grew to the point that in 2010, there were 46 states in the U.S. along with the District of Columbia, Puerto Rico and the U.S. Virgin Islands that had enacted data breach notification laws. These laws basically state that if a state's resident's "personal information" is lost or stolen, the responsible entity must report the incident to all potentially affected citizens. To demonstrate the strength of encryption, some of these laws such as California's Civil Code 1798.80-1798.84 contain "safe harbor" provisions whereby a responsible entity may be relieved of the obligation to disclose a data breach if the "personal information" is encrypted.

The U.S. Federal Government recognizes the need to have its agencies adhere to strong security and data protection standards. Not only is cryptographic technology seen as an important element to information security, all Federal agencies are mandated to use the FIPS 140 standard in designing and implementing cryptographic modules in information systems that they operate or are operated for them. Illustrating how important the FIPS 140 standard is viewed, the Federal Information Security Management Act (FISMA) of 2002 [FISMA] eliminated any provisions to waive the mandatory FIPS 140 validation. FIPS 140 precludes the use of un-validated cryptography for the cryptographic protection of sensitive data within Federal government systems. Un-validated cryptography is viewed as providing no protection to the data, as if it were the same as unprotected plaintext.

Value of FIPS 140

Why does the FIPS 140 standard exist and what purpose does it serve? Product vendors will develop cryptographic technologies to protect data. They will implement known, trusted algorithms. They will test their products to their corporate standards and make assertions that their product is "the most secure in the industry" or "meets industry standards." How can customers know for sure what they are purchasing will perform as advertised and as expected? How can they have confidence that the vendor claims are valid? Without some proof, customers would have to take the vendor's word that their claims are true. The FIPS 140 standards and the Cryptographic Module Validation Program (CMVP) provide value to customers by having independent third-parties validate vendor claims against the internationally-accepted FIPS 140 standards.

Customers want confidence that the products they purchase and use will meet their security requirements. Product vendors may assert that they include cryptographic features in their products and employ secure development practices. The level of confidence (or assurance) customers gain from vendor assertions depends on how trustworthy the vendors are. Independent confirmation of those vendor claims by third-party validators can give customers even greater confidence. Customers can gain even more confidence if those independent, third-party validations are performed using open, international standards. Benefits of these types of validations include:

- Examination against recognized industry standard metrics and criteria so customers have some confidence that the measures are complete and relevant
- Standardized validation methods so that customers are guaranteed consistent, unbiased results
- Credibility of the third party is the basis for trusting their results. Third parties that use open processes for standards development and publication of results gain the broadest credibility

Cryptographic testing and validation standards provide a way to do uniform comparisons of products. Having these standards reduces confusion for the customer so that they are not faced with trying to compare products evaluated under different regimes and criteria.

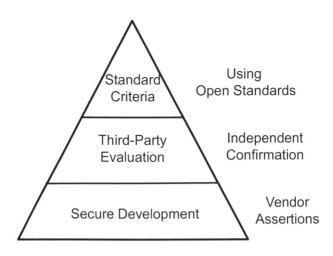

Figure 1: The Assurance Pyramid

The "assurance pyramid" in Figure 1 illustrates the increasing assurance or confidence customers can develop as different validation schemes are applied to assertions about the capabilities of cryptographic modules.

At the base, vendors implement cryptographic technologies in their products and assert that they meet certain standards or have certain capabilities in marketing or advertising claims. These vendors may apply good development practices and do their best to implement solid cryptographic algorithms. If the vendor is trustworthy, customers may be satisfied that their needs will be met.

The second level of assurance is third-party confirmation of vendor claims. This level can provide customers with even greater confidence since this confirmation comes from an independent validator. Depending on how well the third-party is recognized for conducting thorough and accurate validations, the customer may have greater confidence that the cryptography has been developed properly and that the implementation will be free of obvious flaws.

Perhaps the highest level of customer confidence can be gained by the third level of assurance – validation by an independent third-party using open, recognized standards. Open standards allow a broad technical community to contribute to the development of a robust, effective, and realistic set of standards. Customers can gain confidence that a great deal of scrutiny has been placed upon the development of these standards. Customers also have the opportunity to check that the standards will meet their needs. The best standards also include a set of test or validation criteria so that not only is the cryptographic module features well-defined, the methods used to validate them is also specified.

Summary

Encryption has been proven over time to be an effective tool to protect data. Consumers and enterprises have grown to depend on encryption to protect their online transactions and data. Correct implementation and confidence in encryption technologies are important to the continued success of the commercial use of the Internet. Cryptographic module validation programs such as FIPS 140 serve to provide users with a level of confidence that the encryption technologies they use meet industry standards.

Chapter 4: Basic Applied Cryptography

There are a number of the several widely-recognized reference texts available today that cover the technical details of cryptographic algorithms. While the focus of those books is on the mathematics and science of cryptography, describing the gory (and sometimes boring) details of the wide variety of cryptographic techniques used throughout history, the primary purpose of this book is to educate the product developer about the requirements for the current FIPS 140 cryptographic module validation process. However, in order to understand the FIPS 140 validation process, it is necessary to have a basic understanding for the applicable cryptographic technologies recognized by the FIPS 140 standard. This chapter will give the reader that basic understanding using layman's terms and simplified examples.

Encrypting and Decrypting Data

Cryptographic data encryption is rooted in some complex mathematics, however the basic principle is that an algorithm (i.e. mathematical formula) is used to transform (or encode or encrypt) characters or sets of characters (e.g., a plaintext message) into some other form and another algorithm is used to decode (or decrypt) the message back into plaintext. Encryption provides protection of the confidentiality of the messages whereby only authorized recipients are able to read the encrypted messages. In this context, a message may be a message that is transmitted across a network or it can be some data stored on a disk.

A plaintext message can be thought of as nothing but a string of binary digits (bits). ASCII character representations are a common way to transform natural language characters into bits. The letter "A" for example, is represented in ASCII as a hexadecimal 41 or 0100 0001 in binary. The word "America" would then be represented as 41 6D 65 72 69 63 61 in hexadecimal and 0100 0001 0110 1101 0110 0101 0111 0010 0110 1001 0110 0011 0110 0001 in binary. Entering this string into an encoding algorithm results in an encoded bit string (ciphertext). A decoding algorithm and a decoding key are used to reverse the process and decode the ciphertext. Figure 2 illustrates the basic encoding and decoding process.

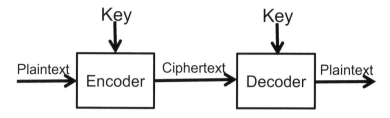

Figure 2: Encoding and Decoding

From a security perspective, it is safer to assume that the encoding and decoding algorithms will become known by attackers, so relying on the secrecy of the algorithms is not prudent. Recognizing this, the FIPS 140-approved algorithms are all documented as open standards and are readily available [CAVP]. Modern cryptographic techniques are so sophisticated that knowing the algorithm alone is not sufficient to decode an encoded message - a "key" must be used. Without the proper key, the encoded message is unintelligible. These "keys" are input parameters to randomize the output and provide the security to the algorithm. Keys have the added advantage that they can easily be changed, making the whole scheme scalable across many users.

A Word About Cryptographic Strength

Cryptographic algorithms are considered "strong" not because they are mathematically impossible to break, but because they are computationally prohibitive to break. Much of the mathematics behind cryptography involves number theory and complex computations. Computations are "expensive" – that is, they take time to compute, so the assumption is that an algorithm is "strong enough" if the computations necessary to break the algorithm are prohibitively expensive. The longer it takes to decrypt a message without knowing the key, the stronger the algorithm is considered to be. If an attacker takes literally years to decrypt an encoded message, it is likely that it would not be worth the effort.

FIPS 140 has selected a set of algorithms that are considered by experts to be strong given today's computing capabilities. Chapter 5: FIPS 140 Approved Algorithms will go into more details about each algorithm that has been approved for the FIPS 140 validation program.

Symmetric Key Algorithms

Figure 2 shows the generic message encoding and decoding process using keys. With symmetric key algorithms, the key used to encode the message is the same as the key used to decode the message, as illustrated in Figure 3. Generally speaking, symmetric key algorithms are simpler and thus less computationally intensive than other algorithms (such as asymmetric algorithms) and are ideal for limited computing platforms such as smart cards or mobile devices. Symmetric key algorithms are also relatively fast, so securing real-time message transfers would be an appropriate application for a symmetric key algorithm.

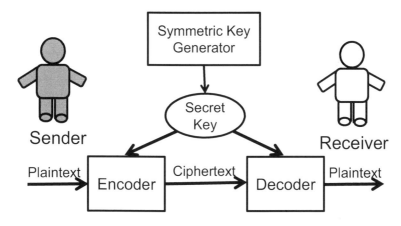

Figure 3: Symmetric Key Algorithm

The major drawback to symmetric key algorithms is that the encoding/decoding key must somehow be securely shared between the sender and the receiver. Asymmetric key algorithms were developed to overcome this shortcoming.

Asymmetric Key Algorithms

Where symmetric key algorithms use the same key for both encoding and decoding data, asymmetric key algorithms use one key for encoding and a different key for decoding. Asymmetric key algorithms are also known as public key algorithms because one key can be shared widely. The other private key must not be distributed. This eliminates the need for a secure mechanism to share keys as with symmetric key algorithms. Freedom from this limitation allows asymmetric methods to be more easily and more widely deployed.

Figure 4 illustrates the asymmetric key algorithm. First, the public key and paired private key are created by the key generator. While the two keys are related, the private key cannot be derived from the public key. The public key may be distributed, so anyone can use it to securely encode messages intended only for the holder of the private key. Only the private key can decode messages encoded using the public key.

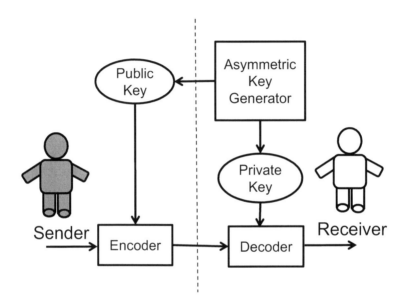

Figure 4: Asymmetric Key Algorithm

A drawback to asymmetric algorithms is that they are more compute-intensive and take longer to operate compared to symmetric key algorithms. For this reason, asymmetric key algorithms may be appropriate for securing email messages where servers and desktops have the necessary computing power and email delivery is less time-sensitive.

Hash Functions

Encrypting messages ensures the confidentiality of the messages. In some applications, all that is needed is to know that the integrity of the message content has been maintained – that is, no one has tampered with the contents of the message. An example of a good application of a cryptographic hash function is verifying a correct and complete file transfer. Hash functions provide message integrity. Figure 5 illustrates how a hash function generates a unique number (hash value or message digest) from a message. The hash function is designed such that the original message cannot be obtained by the hash value - that is, the hashing function is a "one-way" function. The hash value is sent with the message to the receiver. The receiver will re-generate the hash value using the hash function and compare the newly-generated hash value with the hash value that was delivered with the message. If the two values are not equal, then the message was modified in transit.

Figure 5: Hash Function

There is no guarantee that if the two hash values were equal that the message was not modified because the hash function is publicly known and the transmitted hash value is unprotected. Someone could intercept the message, modify the message, create a new hash value and send the modified message with the modified hash value to the original recipient. Hash functions provide no authentication.

Message Authentication Code

Message Authentication Code (MAC) schemes apply a secret (symmetric) key to the transmitted message. This provides the authentication that the message originated from the expected sender. Figure 6 illustrates the MAC scheme mechanism. The sender sends not only the plain text message to the receiver, but a tag is also sent. The tag is generated using the plaintext and the shared secret key as inputs to the MAC algorithm. The receiver then re-generates the tag using the plaintext and the secret key. If the received tag and the re-generated tag are identical, then the plaintext message was not modified and was sent by an authorized entity.

Hash Message Authentication Code (HMAC) appends a symmetric key to the plaintext message prior to generating the hash value. The receiver verifies the originator by re-generating the hash value using the secret key.

Cipher-Block Chaining-Message Authentication Code (CBC-MAC) method encrypts a message using a symmetric key algorithm in cipher-block chaining mode (CBC mode). The last cipher block is used as the message authentication code (MAC). The plaintext and the MAC are both sent. The receiver encrypts the plaintext using the symmetric key to re-generate the last cipher block and compares it to the MAC.

Encrypting messages in fixed-length blocks is called cipher block encryption. Cipher-Block Chaining (CBC) uses a method that causes the decryption of a block of ciphertext to depend on all the preceding ciphertext blocks. A single bit error in a given ciphertext block invalidates the decryption of all subsequent blocks. Rearrangement of the order of the ciphertext blocks corrupts the decryption. This makes it an effective means to detect message tampering.

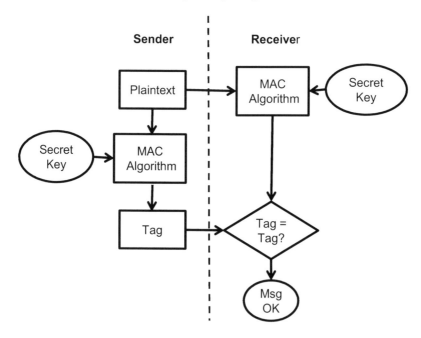

Figure 6: Message Authentication Mechanism

Digital Signatures

A digital signature is a hash value that has been encrypted using an asymmetric algorithm private key. As illustrated in Figure 7, a hash value is computed on the plaintext message using a one-way hash function. The hash value is then encrypted using a private key. The plaintext message, along with the encrypted key is send to the receiver. The receiver then computes the hash value of the plaintext, decrypts the encrypted hash value using the public key, and compares the two values. If the two values are the same, the receiver can be assured that the message came from the expected sender and has not been modified in transit.

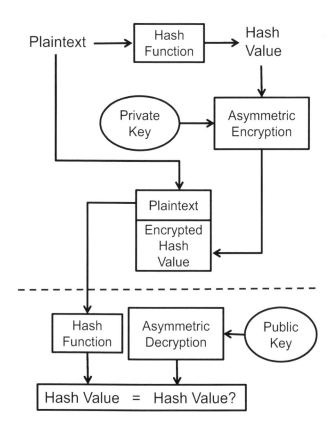

Figure 7: Digital Signature

Digital signatures have the additional benefit of non-repudiation over message authentication codes. Because only one authorized sender can have the asymmetric private key and because the digital signature can only be generated using the private key, the receiver can be assured that the message was sent by only the authorized entity.

Summary of Message Security Options

As discussed so far in this chapter, there are several options to secure messages (and data at rest). Table 1 is a summary of those options and the security features that each provides:

- Encryption provides message confidentiality
- Hashing provides message integrity
- Message authentication provides integrity and authentication
- Digital signatures provide integrity, authentication, and non-repudiation

	Confident-iality	Integrity	Authen-tication	Non-Repudiation
Encryption	X			
Hashing		X		
MAC		X	X	
Digital Signatures		X	X	X

Table 1: Cryptographic Features

Key Generation and Establishment

Since the security and strength of a cryptographic algorithm depends upon the key, key generation and key establishment are critical factors to the quality of the overall cryptographic scheme.

Random Number Generation

Preventing an attacker from guessing cryptographic keys is critical to the success of the cryptographic algorithm. Attackers obtaining secret keys in symmetric key algorithms or private keys in asymmetric algorithms would allow them to read and modify encrypted messages rendering the communications useless. Key generation mechanisms must make it difficult for anyone to guess the keys.

Randomness is an important factor in generating strong keys for cryptographic algorithms. Since keys must be generated from a finite set of possibilities (based on key length), the key generation mechanism must randomly select keys from that set. For example, if the key length is 128 bits long, there are 2^{128} possible keys that can be generated. Strong key generation mechanisms will randomly select a key from the 2^{128} possibilities.

Random number generators are used to help "seed" or start the key generation mechanism. Modern random number generators rely upon entropy or some physical phenomenon that is unpredictable. Some random number generators use ambient air temperature or biometrics as entropy input.

Once a random number has been generated, each key generation algorithm uses its own method for creating the key from the set of all possible keys.

Key Establishment Schemes

As was mentioned earlier in this chapter, symmetric key algorithms have the advantage of being computationally faster and thus requiring less computing power. However, the disadvantage to these algorithms is that the shared, secret key must somehow be distributed in a secure manner in order to be practical. Secret keys can be distributed securely by using a hybrid encryption method that employs asymmetric key algorithms.

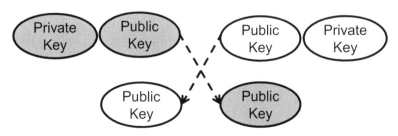

Figure 8: Asymmetric Key Sharing

Figure 8 shows the public and private keys of two parties wishing to share encrypted information. Each party provides the other party with their asymmetric public key.

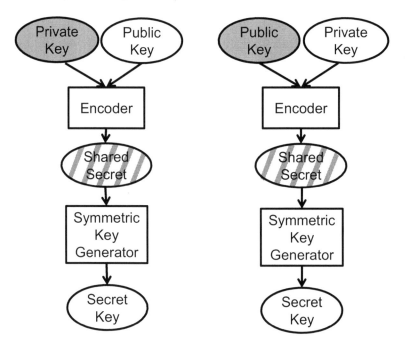

Figure 9: Key Establishment

Figure 9 shows each party using the other party's public key plus their own private key to generate a "shared secret." That shared secret, in turn, is used to generate a symmetric key or secret key. Now that both parties have the secret key, they may communicate with messages encrypted with the symmetric key algorithm.

Cryptography Vulnerabilities

Within each category, the National Institute of Standards and Technology (NIST) approve only a small set of cryptographic algorithms for FIPS 140 validation. The list of approved algorithms has changed over the years as vulnerabilities were discovered in the older ones and new, stronger, more secure algorithms took their places.

Older cryptographic algorithms are replaced as vulnerabilities or weaknesses are discovered. Oftentimes these weaknesses are theoretical mathematical proofs, while others are actual demonstrations of algorithms being broken. In 1999, Distributed.Net and the Electronic Frontier Foundation demonstrated that the then-popular Data Encryption Standard (DES) algorithm could be broken in a matter of hours [RSA DES]. They used a network of nearly 100,000 distributed computers to perform the massive number of calculations necessary to decrypt a DES-encrypted message. As computing power increases and attack techniques grow in sophistication, older algorithms need to be upgraded or replaced in order to maintain the highest levels of security.

Implementation flaws are a major cause for concern with cryptographic modules. Many times cryptographic modules are broken because of software bugs or weak key generation. According to NIST, in 2002 security flaws were discovered during testing in 88 out of 332 algorithms (or 26.5%). By 2010, the error rate had dropped to approximately 10%.

Summary

There are many facets to cryptography including encryption, decryption, hashing, message authentication, digital signatures and key generation. The FIPS 140 reference standards for certain aspects of cryptography. This chapter has provided a basic overview of the cryptographic topics relevant to FIPS 140.

The next set of chapters contained within Part 2 of this book delves into the details of the FIPS 140 standards and the cryptographic algorithm and module validation programs.

PART 2: FIPS 140 OVERVIEW

In this part:

Chapter 5: Algorithm Validation

Chapter 4: Basic Applied Cryptography presented an overview and some of the basic concepts of cryptography highlighting some of the important technologies and how they are used. Product developers certainly need to understand the intricacies and the details of cryptography and the mathematical algorithms behind them in order to implement them properly. Product managers, program managers, and business managers need to know what cryptographic functions are used for and how they affect product functionality. These managers will also need to know what functions are recognized and required by FIPS 140. This chapter will review the Cryptographic Algorithm Validation Program (CAVP) and the specific algorithms recognized in FIPS 140.

Cryptographic Algorithm Validation Program

As a prerequisite for a FIPS 140 validation, a module developer must implement FIPS-approved algorithms and have them validated to ensure each algorithm conforms to their applicable standards. Each approved algorithm has an associated validation suite which specifies test vectors and data report formats required to verify the implementation. Algorithm testing is basically a set of black-box tests run against the respective validation suite to ensure conformance. That is, for a given algorithm, there are a defined set of input test "vectors" that the implementation must accept, process, and produce a result. The result must match the expected result in order to pass the test. Efficient testing of algorithms or implementations of previously-validated cryptographic algorithms can reduce the time to complete the module validation.

The applicable cryptographic algorithm standards can be found on the NIST CAVP website [CAVP] along with sets of example test vectors product vendors can use to test their algorithms prior to the formal validation. The validation is a standalone activity from the cryptographic module validation. The algorithm validation is a prerequisite for module validation, but the algorithm can be validated independent of the module validation.

The CAVP was established by the U.S. National Institute of Standards and Technology (NIST) and the Communications Security Establishment of Canada (CSEC) to oversee cryptographic algorithm tests conducted on FIPS-approved and NIST-recommended cryptographic algorithms. Like the Cryptographic Module Validation Program (CMVP), the CAVP testing is performed by accredited third-party Cryptographic and Security Testing (CST) laboratories.

As Figure 10 illustrates, the algorithm validation process should begin before the module validation. However, the module validation may begin before the algorithm validation is complete. The algorithm validation should be completed before the module testing phase has completed (more on that in Chapter 6: Module Validation.)

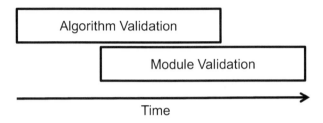

Figure 10: Algorithm Validation Prerequisite

Algorithm Validation Process

The CAVP defines a set of tests for each FIPS 140-approved cryptographic algorithm. As a prerequisite to the cryptographic module validation portion of the FIPS 140 validation, the algorithms implemented within the cryptographic module must pass the applicable algorithm tests. These tests are referred to as the "algorithm validation suites." Algorithm validation suites (AVS) are sets of functional tests designed to verify the correct implementation of the specified cryptographic algorithm.

The NIST CAVP website [CAVP] has links to the various AVS for each FIPS 140-approved algorithm along with sample test vectors. Product developers can use these sample test vectors to pre-test their implementations to check for compliance prior to the formal validation. However, the actual test vectors used during the validation will be generated by the cryptographic testing lab. The product developer will use these test vectors to run the tests. The product developer will then send the test results to the testing lab for verification. Finally, NIST CAVP validates the results and issues the algorithm certificate. The NIST website publishes the list of certified algorithms [CAVL]. Figure 11 illustrates the complete algorithm validation process overview.

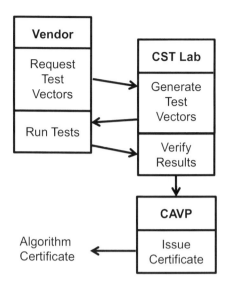

Figure 11: CAVP Process Overview

FIPS 140 Approved Algorithms

The CAVP validation is done by executing functional tests on the cryptographic algorithm, recording the results, and validating the results against expected results. The NIST CAVP website [CAVP] has references to not only the standard algorithm definitions but also to documents detailing the test procedures and sample test suites that can be used to verify the algorithm implementations. Product developers can use these documents as guidance to help ensure a successful CAVP validation on their way towards a FIPS 140 module validation.

The cryptographic categories that are covered by CAVP are:

- Symmetric Key Algorithms
- Asymmetric Key Algorithms
- Message Authentication
- Hashing
- Random Number Generators
- Deterministic Random Bit Generators
- Key Management

The following sections in this chapter describe the FIPS 140-approved cryptographic categories, their applicable standards, and the CAVP testing references.

Symmetric Key Algorithms

The main characteristic of symmetric key algorithms is that they use the same keys for both encryption and decryption. Symmetric key algorithms are also known as shared key, private key or secret key algorithms. These algorithms are known by these names because the key is shared between the parties transferring messages and must keep the key secret or private in order to ensure security.

There are two types of symmetric key algorithms – block ciphers and stream ciphers. A block cipher encodes and decodes messages in fixed-length blocks while a stream cipher handles message content byte-by-byte.

The main advantage of symmetric key algorithms is that they are relatively computationally simple and quick and are used for encrypting large messages for transmission. The major drawback to this method is finding a way to securely distribute the shared key to the sender(s) and receiver(s).

There are currently three FIPS 140-approved symmetric key algorithms. They are:

- Advanced Encryption Standard "Rijndael"(AES)
- Triple Data Encryption Algorithm "Triple DES" (TDEA)
- Escrowed Encryption Standard "Skipjack" (EES)

Advanced Encryption Standard (AES)

The Advanced Encryption Standard (AES) is detailed in NIST Federal Information Processing Standard (FIPS) Publication 197 [FIPS 197]. AES uses the symmetric key block cipher Rijndael algorithm [Rijndael] using key lengths of 128, 192 and 256 bits.

The Rijndael cipher was developed by two Belgian cryptographers, Joan Daemen and Vincent Rijmen and was adopted by the U.S. National Institute of Standards and Technology (NIST) in late 2001 and replaced the Data Encryption Standard [DES] (formerly FIPS 46-3) in 2005.

The XOR-Encrypt-XOR Tweakable CodeBook mode encryption with ciphertext stealing (XTS-AES) is an alternative mode of operation recognized by NIST for the AES algorithm. NIST SP 800-38E [SP 800-38E] describes XTS-AES as a narrow-block cryptographic mode. The XTS-AES mode is a version of Peter Rogaway's XOR-Encrypt-XOR (XOX) block cipher. The XTS-AES mode was developed to protect data storage devices that use fixed length data units.

AES uses the substitution permutation network (SPN) to create the ciphertext. DES used the Feistel network which has a smaller computing footprint and may be more applicable for smart cards or other lower computing powered devices. SPN can take advantage of the parallelism in general-purpose computers to achieve higher throughput.

AES tests are described in the Advanced Encryption Standard Algorithm Validation Suite [AESAVS] document. The AESAVS provides descriptions for configuration, known answer tests, multi-block message tests, and Monte Carlo tests. The validation tests for the XTS-AES are described in the XTS-AES Validation System [XTSVS] document.

Triple Date Encryption Algorithm (TDEA)

The Data Encryption Standard (DES) was a popular block cipher using a 56-bit key but was replaced as a FIPS 140-approved cryptographic algorithm primarily due to its relatively short key length by the AES. The Triple Data Encryption Algorithm (TDEA), also commonly referred to as "Triple DES", is an accepted algorithm and basically applies DES three times to each message block. TDEA is detailed in NIST Special Publication 800-67 [TDEA].

NIST Special Publication 800-38A [SP 800-38A] Appendix E references the block cipher modes of Triple-DES while ANSI X9.52-1998 [ANSI] documents the TDEA modes of operation.

Triple-DES known answer tests are described in NIST Special Publication 800-20 [SP 800-20] and the Multi-block Message Tests [MMT] documents.

Escrowed Encryption Standard (EES)

The Escrowed Encryption Standard (EES) or "Skipjack" is referenced in NIST FIPS 185 [FIPS 185] and specified in *Skipjack and KEA*

Algorithm Specifications [Skipjack]. The Skipjack algorithm is a symmetric key algorithm using an 80-bit key to encrypt 64-bit blocks.

Skipjack tests are described in NIST Special Publication 800-17, [SP 800-17]. The tests described in SP 800-17 are known answer tests for encryption and decryption using several modes of operation.

Asymmetric Key Algorithms

Asymmetric key algorithms are also known as public key algorithms. These algorithms are different from symmetric key algorithms in that a widely-distributed public key is used to encode the plaintext while only a private key can be used to decode the ciphertext. This eliminates the need for a secure mechanism to share keys as with symmetric key algorithms. Freedom from this limitation allows asymmetric methods to be more easily and more widely deployed. The CAVP recognizes the use of asymmetric key algorithms for digital signatures. Digital signatures provide origin authentication, data integrity, and signer non-repudiation.

NIST FIPS 186-3 [FIPS 186-3] describes the Digital Signature Standard (DSS). FIPS 186-3 supersedes FIPS 186-2 and specifies the use of hash functions included in the Secure Hash Standard FIPS 180-3 [FIPS 180-3] and not just SHA-1 as specified in FIPS 186-2.

DSS references SP 800-57 [SP 800-57] for guidance on key management including the key sizes to be used. NIST SP 800-90 [SP 800-90] is the reference for random number generation using deterministic random bit generators.

The 3 FIPS 140-approved digital signature generation and verification algorithms are:

- Digital Signature Algorithm (DSA)
- Rivest, Shamir, Adleman Algorithm (RSA)
- Elliptic Curve Digital Signature Algorithm (ECDSA)

The Digital Signature Algorithm Validation System [DSAVS] describes the DSA algorithm validation testing requirements for FIPS 186-3. The RSA Validation System [RSAVS] covers the RSA validation testing for FIPS 186-2. The Elliptic Curve Digital Signature Algorithm Validation System [ECDSAVS] details the ECDSA testing.

SSL/TLS, HTTPS and IPSec

Secure Socket Layer (SSL) is a well-known security protocol developed by Netscape Corporation in 1995. SSL and its successor, the Transport Layer Security (TLS) protocol, use asymmetric key encryption to secure connections across the Internet.

HTTPS is the secure form of Hyper-Text Transfer Protocol (HTTP) whereby HTTPS encrypts webpage requests and responses using SSL/TLS.

Internet Protocol Security (IPSec) is an industry standard protocol for authenticating and encrypting individual packets being transmitted across the Internet.

These are popular security protocols that implement FIPS 140-approved algorithms.

Message Authentication

Message authentication is a means to maintain the integrity of transmitted messages by applying a secret (symmetric) key to the message. The FIPS 140-approved message authentication schemes employ cipher-block chaining or hashing. The FIPS 140-approved methods are:

- Cipher Block Chaining Mode Authentication Code
- Counter with Cipher Block Chaining-Message Authentication Code
- Galois/Counter Mode and GMAC
- Keyed-Hash Message Authentication Code

Cipher Block Chaining Mode Authentication Code

The Cipher Block Chaining Mode Authentication Code (CMAC) is described in NIST Special Publication 800-38B [SP 800-38B]. The testing requirements for this algorithm are in the CMAC Validation System [CMACVS]. The underlying NIST-approved symmetric key algorithm (AES and TDEA) must be validated as part of the CMAC validation.

Counter with Cipher Block Chaining-Message Authentication Code

The Counter with Cipher Block Chaining-Message Authentication Code (CCM) is described in NIST Special Publication 800 38C [SP 800-38C]. CCM is only approved on symmetric key block cipher algorithms whose block size is 128 bits, such as the Advanced Encryption Standard (AES). The testing requirements for this algorithm are in the Counter with Cipher Block Chaining-Message Authentication Code (CCM) Validation System [CCMVS] document.

Galois/Counter Mode and GMAC

The Galois/Counter Mode (GCM) is described in NIST Special Publication 800 38D [SP 800-38D]. GCM is based on an approved symmetric key block cipher algorithm whose block size is 128 bits, such as the Advanced Encryption Standard (AES) – TDEA block size is only 64 bits and thus is not applicable. The Galois/Counter Mode (GCM) and GMAC Validation System [GCMVS] describes the testing requirements for GCM.

Keyed-Hash Message Authentication Code

The Keyed-Hash Message Authentication Code (HMAC) is described in NIST FIPS 198 [FIPS 198]. The Keyed-Hash Message Authentication Code (HMAC) Validation System [HMACVS] document describes the algorithm testing. All of the underlying SHA algorithms supported by the HMAC implementation must be validated as part of the HMAC validation.

Hashing

The Secure Hash Standard is described in NIST FIPS 180-3 [FIPS 180-3] and includes Secure Hash Algorithm-1 (SHA-1), SHA-224, SHA-256, SHA-384, and SHA-512. The Secure Hash Algorithm Validation System [SHAVS] document describes the testing for these algorithms.

Random Number Generators

NIST FIPS 140 Annex C [FIPS 140-2 C] documents the approved random number generators (RNG). A deterministic RNG consists of an algorithm that produces a sequence of bits from an initial value called a seed. A non-deterministic RNG produces output that is dependent on some unpredictable physical source that is outside human control. This standard only calls out deterministic RNGs. No non-deterministic RNGs have been approved. The approved RNGs are documented in the following documents:

1. FIPS Publication 186-3 – Digital Signature Standard [FIPS 186-3]
2. Digital Signatures Using Reversible Public Key Cryptography for the Financial Services Industry, ANSI X9.31-1998 - Appendix A.2.4.[ANSI]
3. Public Key Cryptography for the Financial Services Industry: The Elliptic Curve Digital Signature Algorithm (ECDSA), ANSI X9.62-1998 – Annex A.4. [ANSI]
4. NIST-Recommended Random Number Generator Based on ANSI X9.31 Appendix A.2.4 Using the 3-Key Triple DES and AES Algorithms [NIST RNG]
5. Recommendation for Random Number Generation Using Deterministic Random Bit Generators, Special Publication 800-90 [SP 800-90].

The random number generator testing requirements are documented in the Random Number Generator Validation System [RNGVS].

Deterministic Random Bit Generators

FIPS 140-approved deterministic random bit generators (DRBG) are documented in NIST SP 800-90 [SP 800-90]. The four mechanisms included in SP 800-90 are based on either hash functions, block cipher algorithms using counter mode, or number theoretic problems.

The testing requirements for DRBG can be found in the DRBG Validation System [DRBGVS] document.

Key Management

NIST SP 800-56A [SP 800-56A] specifies the FIPS 140-approved key establishment schemes. SP 800-56A is based on ANSI X9.42, *Agreement of Symmetric Keys Using Discrete Logarithm Cryptography* and ANSI X9.63, *Key Agreement and Key Transport Using Elliptic Curve Cryptography*.

The testing requirements for this algorithm can be found in the Key Agreement Schemes Validation System document [KASVS]. The KASVS validation process also requires testing of the supported DSA and/or ECDSA, SHA algorithm(s), MAC algorithm(s), and the RNG and/or DRBG algorithm(s).

Summary

Tables 2 through 7 summarize the FIPS 140-approved algorithms and the applicable standard documents.

Cryptographic Technology	Applicable Standard
AES	FIPS 197
Triple-DES	SP 800-67
EES	FIPS 185

Table 2: Symmetric Key Standards

Cryptographic Technology	Applicable Standard
DSA, RSA, ECDSA	FIPS 186-3
DSS	FIPS 186-2

Table 3: Asymmetric Key Standards

Cryptographic Technology	Applicable Standard
HMAC	FIPS 198
CMAC	SP 800-38B
CCM	SP 800-38C
GMC and GMAC	SP 800-38D

Table 4: MAC Standards

Cryptographic Technology	Applicable Standard
SHA-1, 224, 256, 384, 512	FIPS 180-3

Table 5: Hash Standards

Cryptographic Technology	Applicable Standard
RNG for DSA	FIPS 186-2
RNG for ECDSA	ANSI X.9-62
RNG for RSA	ANSI X.9-31
DRBG	SP 800-90

Table 6: Random Number Generator Standards

Cryptographic Technology	Applicable Standard
KAS FCC and KAS ECC	SP 800-56A

Table 7: Key Management Standards

65

Chapter 6: Module Validation

Chapter 4: Basic Applied Cryptography of this book provided the basics of cryptography and the specific cryptographic algorithms approved by the National Institute of Standards and Technology (NIST) and the Communications Security Establishment of Canada (CSEC). The previous chapter (Chapter 5: Algorithm Validation) described the validation process for those approved algorithms. However, the core of the FIPS 140 validation is the module validation. The module validation is intended to verify that the module under test meets the FIPS 140 standards. The testing lab will verify that the necessary security features have been implemented correctly and that the standard security requirements have been met.

This chapter introduces the FIPS 140 module validation process and provides an overview of the requirements for a successful validation.

Cryptographic Module Validation Program

Federal Information Processing Standard 140 (FIPS 140) specifies requirements for cryptographic modules. Product vendors pursue this rigorous standard to sell products to U.S. Federal government departments and agencies and other industry vertical markets. FIPS 140 specifies requirements for hardware and software products that implement cryptographic functionality as well as the testing requirements to validate conformance claims. FIPS 140 is applicable to all Federal agencies that use cryptographic-based security systems to protect sensitive and unclassified information in computer and telecommunication systems as defined in Section 5131 of the Information Technology Management Reform Act of 1996.

The mandate for FIPS 140 stems from the National Security Telecommunications and Information Systems Security Policy (NSTISSP) Number 11. This policy requires the use of only approved information assurance products in systems that enter, process, store, display, or transmit national security information. Approved products are those validated against the International Common Criteria for Information Security Technology (Common Criteria) or FIPS 140.

The Cryptographic Module Validation Program (CMVP), the body which owns and manages the FIPS 140 validation program, is a joint effort between U.S. National Institute of Standards and Technology (NIST) and the Communications Security Establishment of Canada (CSEC). Validations are performed by independent, third-party commercial testing laboratories. These cryptographic and security testing (CST) labs are accredited by NIST's National Voluntary Laboratory Accreditation Program (NVLAP).

In addition to drafting the requirements and validating test reports, the CMVP also maintains a list of products that are either pursuing validation or have completed validation. Procurement officials in Federal agencies refer to these lists when making purchasing decisions. While most agencies are able to purchase products that are in the process of testing, not all agencies do so. This practice varies according to different procurement policies set by each agency.

FIPS 140-1 was made into a mandatory standard in 1994. As of 2001, FIPS 140-2 is the current revision and supersedes FIPS 140-1. Vendors were able to pursue FIPS 140-1 validations until May 2002, and agencies were able to continue to purchase and use FIPS 140-1 validated modules after the transition. The newest revision of the standard, FIPS 140-3, is currently in development and there is no specified date of release at the time of this writing. FIPS 140 is also recognized in the international standards area as:

- ISO/IEC 19790 Security Requirements for Cryptographic Modules
- ISO/IEC 24759 Test requirements for cryptographic modules

Motivation to Pursue FIPS 140 Validation

As previously mentioned, FIPS 140 validation is required to sell products implementing cryptography to the U.S. Federal government. The single largest reason for a vendor to pursue FIPS 140 is to be able to sell products to the United States Federal agencies. As requirements for FIPS 140 develop in the finance industry and international government markets, vendors will likely pursue FIPS 140 validation to remain competitive in the global security market.

Vendors also pursue FIPS 140 validation to provide security assurance for a product's cryptographic functionality. The validation process requires third-party testing and evaluation of algorithm implementations, key management, and other cryptographic features and functions covered under the FIPS 140 requirements. Completing the validation process proves to potential customers in the public or private sector that the cryptographic module was designed according to stringent requirements adopted by the U.S. Federal government. The assurance of a FIPS 140 validation reduces risk for purchasing agents because the product was thoroughly tested by an independent testing laboratory.

A couple of notable government customer programs require FIPS 140 validations. The U.S. Army organizations are instructed to purchase only products listed on the Information Assurance Approved Products List (IAAPL). A FIPS 140 validation is required of all products containing cryptographic modules in order to be listed in the IAAPL. The latest "letter to Industry" [Army2009] from the U.S. Army detailed updated cryptographic module requirements pertaining to FIPS 140-2 validations. The requirements stated in the letter were:

- Software-only modules validated at FIPS 140-2 Overall Level 1 must have Roles, Services and Authentication at level 2 and Design Assurance at level 3
- Hardware, firmware and hybrid modules must be validated to FIPS 140-2 Overall Level 2 and must have Cryptographic Module and Design Assurance at level 3
- Mobile devices, smart phones, PDAs, USB memory devices, and encrypted flash drives must be validated to FIPS 140-2 Overall Level 2 and must have Roles, Services and Authentication at level 3

Another U.S. military testing program is the Defense Information Systems Agency's (DISA) Joint Interoperability Test Command (JITC). JITC performs certification testing on products and systems to be deployed in U.S. Department of Defense organizations. JITC requires any product containing a cryptographic module to have a FIPS 140 validation.

Module Validation Statistics

To illustrate the popularity and growth of the CMVP, Randall Easter, NIST CMVP director, in March 2010 reported that there were 1264 FIPS 140-1 and FIPS 140-2 completed validations representing over 2624 modules [Easter 2010]. At that time there were over 305 vendors of validated modules. Figure 12 was generated using data from the validated products list [CMVL] and illustrates the number of validated modules by year and validation level (1-4).

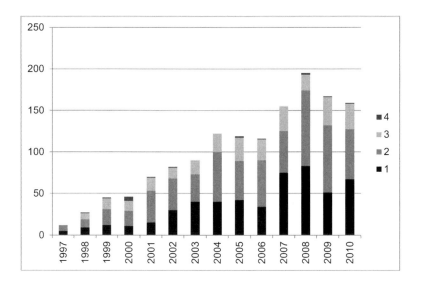

Figure 12: Validated Modules by Year and Level

Randall Easter also reported that many of the cryptographic modules surveyed during testing contained at least one non-conformance error. This illustrates the effectiveness of the testing to identify issues with the cryptographic modules that might have compromised customers' data and systems. Below are the percentages of modules with at least one non-conformance issue discovered during testing.

- 59% in level 1 and level 2 validations
- 65% in level 3 and level 4 validations
- 96.3% in FIPS interpretation and documentation errors
- Approximately 10% in algorithm implementation errors

The low percentage (10%) of the modules with algorithm implementation errors seems to indicate that algorithm implementation is not much of an issue for product developers. The developers seem to be able to follow the algorithm standards and implement them properly. However, Easter reported that the areas of greatest difficulty seemed to be in the areas of:

- Key Management
- Physical Security
- Self Tests
- Random Number Generation

FIPS 140-validated cryptographic modules are categorized into one of three configurations or embodiments. The physical security requirements for each embodiment are different. The physical security requirements are discussed in greater detail in Chapter 8: Security Requirements. The three embodiments are:

- Single Chip
- Multi-Chip Embedded
- Multi-Chip Standalone

A cryptographic module is classified as a single chip configuration when the module is enclosed within a single integrated circuit (IC). A multi-chip embedded module such as a peripheral component interconnect (PCI) card can be enclosed in a protective case and is used in a host device or platform. A multi-chip standalone configuration includes security appliances and software running on general-purpose computing hardware. Figure 13 illustrates the breakdown of validated modules by hardware, software or firmware and their embodiments.

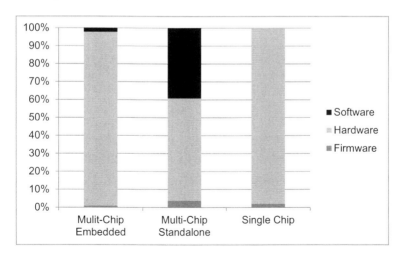

Figure 13: Module Embodiments

71

Module Validation Process

As Figure 14 illustrates, the FIPS 140 validation process is comprised of three main phases: the Documentation Phase, the Implementation Under Test Phase, and the Validation Phase. The Validation Phase is broken down into four sub-phases: Review Pending, Validation Review, Validation Coordination, and Validation Finalization.

CMVP reports the status of modules in the Implementation Under Test and Validation Phases on the CMVP Modules In Process website [MIP]. The status is reported according to the phase the module is currently in.

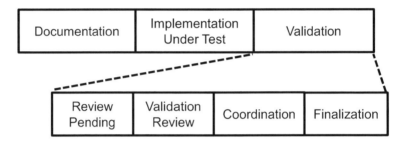

Figure 14: Module Validation Phases

Documentation Phase

The cryptographic module under test must be thoroughly documented to address FIPS 140 requirements, and supporting assurance documentation must be developed to support vendor claims of conformance.

Not only does the FIPS 140 validation require correct implementation of the approved cryptographic algorithms with the standard security features (see Chapter 8: Security Requirements), FIPS 140 module validation also requires extensive, specialized documentation to address the FIPS 140 requirements. Most of this documentation is typically not produced as part of a vendor's normal product and documentation development processes. There are three main documents required by FIPS 140 testing laboratories:

1.   Security Policy
2.   Vendor Evidence
3.   Finite State Model

Category	Addresses these questions:
Cryptographic Module Specifications	What is the cryptographic boundary (e.g., what is being tested)?
Cryptographic Module Ports and Interfaces	What are the physical and logical interfaces of the cryptographic boundary?
Roles, Services, and Authentication	What roles are available in the module? What are the services for those roles, and how are those roles authenticated?
Finite State Model	What are the discrete states for the module? What are the state transitions, and what services are available in each state?
Physical Security	How is the cryptographic boundary physically protected from modification?
Operational Environment	What is the operational environment (e.g., limited, general purpose) of the cryptographic module?
Cryptographic Key Management	What keys exist in the module and how are they generated, stored, used, and deleted?
Electro-Magnetic Interference / Compatibility (EMI/EMC)	Has the module under test been submitted for FCC testing for EMI/EMC and to which class was the module tested?
Self-Tests	How does the module ensure integrity of components and proper functionality of cryptographic algorithms?
Design Assurance	How was the module designed and developed? What processes were used for configuration management and secure delivery?
Mitigation of Other Attacks	Does the module attempt to mitigate attacks not addressed in the FIPS 140 standard?

Table 8: Security Requirement Categories

The Security Policy document provides an introduction to the module, a high-level summary of how the module meets the FIPS 140 requirements, and the validation level. Since many modules require special configuration to meet FIPS 140 requirements, the Security Policy also provides instructions on how to initialize and operate the module in the FIPS-approved mode of operation. This document is non-proprietary and is posted on the CMVP website with the module's validation certificate.

The Vendor Evidence documents address the FIPS 140 Security Requirements and provide a basis of input for the report from the cryptographic and security testing (CST) laboratory. These documents provide detailed descriptions of how the module meets each requirement in each applicable section of FIPS 140 for the specified validation level. Chapter 8: Security Requirements describes, in detail, the FIPS 140 security requirements, but the 11 Security Requirements categories are shown in Table 8.

The Finite State Model (FSM) documents the module's states and transitions and augments Section 4 of the Derived Test Requirements (DTR). This document also addresses services available in each state.

These documents are further supported by additional documentation to support the claims of the vendor. For example, other supporting documents in a validation submission package can include the following: Federal Communications Commission (FCC) certificates for Electro-Magnetic Interference/Electro-Magnetic Compatibility (EMI/EMC) compliance, the master components list, schematics, block diagrams, configuration management plans, and source code listings for all software and firmware within the cryptographic boundary.

Implementation Under Test Phase

To begin the Implementation Under Test (IUT) Phase, the documentation and module under test are submitted to an accredited FIPS 140 testing laboratory. To formally launch the IUT Phase, a viable contract must exist between the vendor and CST laboratory for the testing of the cryptographic module. The laboratory will evaluate the documentation and test the module against the FIPS 140 requirements. During this phase, the documentation may be updated or reworked based on unresolved issues or comments from the testing laboratory.

When the CST lab completes the testing, it submits the results to the CMVP. At that point, the module enters the Validation Review Pending Phase.

Validation Review Pending Phase

To enter the Validation Review Pending Phase, the CST lab has successfully completed the evaluation of the documentation, validation of algorithms, and testing of the product functionality against FIPS 140 requirements. The testing lab submits a complete set of testing documents to CMVP for review. The documentation includes: the draft certificate, the summary module description, the detailed test report, the Security Policy document and a letter of recommendation from the testing laboratory.

Modules In Process List

A vendor may be listed (at their option) on the NIST Modules In Process website [MIP] when the product(s) and the FIPS 140 documentation package has been submitted to a testing laboratory. The Modules In Process website tracks modules through all of the major validation phases: Implementation Under Test, Validation Review Pending, Validation Review, Validation Coordination, and Validation Finalization.

Federal agencies are required to purchase cryptographic products that have been FIPS 140 validated. Many end users cannot wait for a product to complete the lengthy FIPS 140 process before deploying software/equipment in mission-critical situations. As such, many agencies purchase products that are listed on the FIPS 140 Modules In Process list. The CMVP created the Modules In Process list as a formal listing of which products are in the process of pursuing FIPS 140 validation. Since agencies can purchase products on the FIPS 140 Modules In Process list, timely completion of the documentation and submission to a testing laboratory is an important milestone for product vendors.

From this phase forward, there is little work the product vendor has to do except to sit and wait for the reviewers to complete their work.

Validation Review Phase

At the Validation Review Phase, NIST and CSEC reviewers are assigned. NIST and CSEC perform a preliminary review of the test documents and perform a review of the test documents. Any reviewer comments are sent to the CST laboratory.

Validation Coordination Phase

During the Validation Coordination Phase, the CST lab resolves the comments received from NIST and CSEC reviewers. The CST lab performs any additional testing that may be required to properly address the reviewers' comments. Additional documentation may need to be developed to address the reviewers' comments. Once all of the comments have been addressed, the resolutions including documentation and updated test results are prepared for re-submission to the NIST and CSEC reviewers.

Validation Finalization Phase

The Validation Finalization Phase brings final resolution to the validation review comments reported by the NIST and CSEC reviewers. The FIPS 140 certificate number is assigned by CMVP and the certificate printing and signature process is initiated.

Once the certificate has been issued, the module information will be listed on the NIST Module Validation List [CMVL].

Summary

The FIPS 140 validation is an important requirement to selling products containing cryptographic functionality to U.S. Federal government customers. Federal agencies are mandated to purchase only FIPS 140-validated modules to protect their sensitive, but unclassified data and systems.

The FIPS 140 validation process is overseen by NIST's Cryptographic Module Validation Program using independent third-party testing labs accredited by NIST's National Voluntary Laboratory Accreditation Program.

The FIPS 140 validation process involves several phases including:

- Implementation Under Test
- Validation Review Pending
- Validation Review
- Validation Coordination
- Validation Finalization

Throughout the validation process, there are several key documents that are developed specifically for the FIPS 140 validation including:

- Security Policy
- Vendor Evidence
- Finite State Model

The next chapter of this book will describe the costs and timelines of the FIPS 140 module validation process.

Chapter 7: Costs and Timelines

Product vendors are responsible for delivering robust, high-quality, and timely products to their customers. Product vendors wishing to sell products to customers concerned with the integrity of the cryptographic functionality within these products are also responsible for obtaining FIPS 140 validations. Product vendors are responsible for assuming the burden of the costs associated with these validations and may hire outside consulting expertise to help in the development and documentation of the cryptographic module. The vendor will employ an accredited testing lab to conduct the validation testing and will pay the applicable government fees.

This significant investment in time and money requires sound planning. Understanding the total cost and effort investment is the first step in this planning process. This chapter will provide an overview of the roles and responsibilities of all the parties involved, a complete breakdown of the expected costs, and estimated timelines for a FIPS 140 validation.

Roles and Responsibilities

There are four independent parties involved in a FIPS 140 validation project. It is important to understand what role each party plays and what responsibilities they are expected to fulfill toward a successful FIPS 140 validation. The four parties are:

1. Product Developer
2. Consultant
3. Testing Lab
4. Government (CMVP)

Table 9 summarizes the roles and responsibilities of each of the parties involved in the FIPS 140 validation project. The table illustrates the actions and output of each party.

Party	Vendor	Consultant	CST Lab	CMVP
Actions	Designs & Produces	Manages & Guides	Tests for Conformance	Validates
Outputs	Crypto Module	Documents, Strategy	Test Report	Test Results & Issues Certificate

Table 9: Roles and Responsibilities

Product Developer

Product developer must design and develop a cryptographic module that has all of the features necessary to meet the security requirements of the FIPS 140 standards [FIPS 140-2]. The product developer must implement at least one FIPS 140-approved cryptographic algorithm in the module to be tested. The cryptographic module must provide the supporting functionality (such as self-tests and tamper-detection) to meet the FIPS 140 security requirements. The FIPS 140 security requirements also include requirements beyond strict module features such as design assurance which reflects the developer's development, delivery and operational environments. The FIPS 140 security requirements are discussed in detail in Chapter 8: Security Requirements.

The product developer must also provide the technical details about the product to generate the necessary documentation that the testing lab will evaluate against the FIPS 140 requirements. The whole philosophy behind FIPS 140 validations is that customers gain greater assurance about the security of the cryptographic module if an accredited, independent third-party testing lab checks vendors' claims. These tests are conducted using not only the module itself but documentation describing the module as well.

Consultant

The product developer is the sponsor for the FIPS 140 validation project. The sponsor is responsible for paying for the resources necessary to complete the project. Deciding to hire an outside consultant or to use in-house resources will require a "buy-versus-build" analysis by the sponsor. Depending upon the type of services the product vendor desires or the type of help s/he needs, the FIPS 140 consultant may deliver training, conduct assessments, provide design assistance, and/or develop validation strategies. The key service FIPS 140 consultants provide to the product developer is development of evidence documentation.

The FIPS 140 validation process requires that specialized documentation be delivered to the testing lab for their review. These documents are not typically developed during the normal course of product development. There are three main documents that are expected by the testing lab including:

1.   Security Policy
2.   Vendor Evidence
3.   Finite State Model

Competent FIPS 140 consultants know what content the testing labs are expecting in each of these documents. They also are experienced in delivering these documents in formats that are most easily understood by the testing labs. This experience helps reduce the number of questions from the lab and thus reduces the documentation rework efforts. Even if the product developer decides to write some of the documentation themselves, consultants can help by providing guidance to ensure a smooth and efficient validation project.

Testing Lab

The primary role of the cryptographic and security testing (CST) lab is to test the cryptographic module for conformance to the FIPS 140 requirements.

During the prerequisite algorithm testing phase, the CST lab provides the algorithm test vectors to the product developer based on the FIPS 140-approved algorithms contained in the module under test. After the developer has completed the algorithm tests and submitted the results, the CST lab validates the test results.

The CST lab receives the Security Policy, Vendor Evidence and Finite State Model and supporting documentation, and conducts the module tests. The CST lab will return any comments or questions to the product developer for clarification or correction. When all of the comments have been addressed, the CST lab sends their validation test report and recommendation to CMVP.

Government (CMVP)

The CMVP is responsible for the final verification of the test results and issuing the FIPS 140 certificate. Once CMVP receives the reports and documentation from the CST lab, they go through several formal validation phases.

- Validation Review Pending
- Validation Review
- Validation Coordination
- Validation Finalization

CMVP updates their website with the latest status information about current and completed FIPS 140 validations.

Costs

The product vendor is responsible for paying the consultants they hire to assist them in the design and documentation of the cryptographic module. The vendor is also responsible for paying the testing lab to test and validate the cryptographic module against the FIPS 140 standards. There is also a government "cost recovery fee" that is paid by the vendor to offset the costs of the efforts of the CMVP to certify the testing lab results and issue the formal certificate.

Commercial product developers have an obligation to their shareholders to plan for these expenses and to get the best value for their investments. The following sections of this chapter highlight issues product developers should consider when planning a FIPS 140 validation project.

Due Diligence

As the sponsor for the FIPS 140 validation, product developers pay for the entire validation effort. Product developers provide the technical information necessary to create the evidence documentation. They select the validation lab and may elect to hire an outside consultant to create the evidence documentation. The developer pays the bills and is responsible for ensuring that the money is spent wisely.

As with any third-party selection process, product developers pursuing FIPS 140 validations must exercise sound due diligence practices. This means doing some research and setting meaningful selection criteria. Some of the important criteria to consider are:

- Experience and competence of the service providers demonstrated by successful FIPS 140 validations
- Service provider's flexibility when working with product developers
- Timeliness and responsiveness of the service provider to avoid costly delays

In order to constrain and control costs, it is important to get several competitive quotes or estimates from the prospective consultants and validation testing labs. Requests for proposals should request information regarding all of the costs including travel and other expenses.

Price comparison can be difficult for FIPS 140 testing labs and consultants. There is very little public cost data available and what data is available takes time to collect. Product vendors will generally need to request cost estimates and quotes directly from each party individually and will need to be prepared to do some analysis once the cost data from the providers has been made available.

Some providers will deliver quotes while others will only give estimates. Product vendors should read the quotes and estimates carefully and note that estimates are only estimates based on a set of assumptions about the complexity of the validation.

Checking references is an important factor in any due diligence process. Product vendors should ask the providers for as many references as possible. Then they should be sure to check these. Ask the references open ended questions about the general experience they had with the service provider. Then ask more detailed questions about the length of time it took and what issues or problems they encountered and how they resolved them.

Time and Material Versus Fixed-Price Contracts

Consultants and testing labs will typically charge the vendor on a time and materials (T&M) or on a fixed-price basis. How much they charge depends on their experience, overhead and the complexity of the module validation effort.

The danger with T&M contracts is that the more time the service providers spend on reworking or re-assessing documents, the more money the vendor has to spend to complete the validation.

T&M contracts usually make it quite clear what the vendor is paying for. These contracts have all of the itemized details – hourly rate of the resource, overhead, travel and other expenses. If the contract does not have these details, it certainly should. T&M contracts will generally have an estimate for the number of person-hours it will take to complete the project. Some T&M contracts will breakdown the time estimates further by providing estimates on the time to be spent in each phase or work unit. The person-hours are only estimates and if rework is required, the vendor will pay for the additional hours of effort at the contracted rate.

Fixed-price contracts prevent vendors from having to pay extra for rework effort. Fixed-price contracts make budgeting more predictable and also incentivize the service provider to minimize rework; this pushes the provider to do a good job the first time through. However, fixed-price contracts costs are developed assuming some amount of rework will be involved, and a premium could be associated with that.

Consultant Costs

FIPS 140 consultants offer a variety of services to product development vendors. They can offer FIPS 140 training to educate developers on the FIPS 140 security requirements and the FIPS 140 validation process. They may offer certification strategy development services to help guide the product developer toward an efficient and robust strategic product certification plan. Consultants will generally conduct a pre-validation assessment of the target cryptographic module to assess any deficiencies in the product design relative to the FIPS 140 requirements. They can also provide more specific design guidance on how to rectify any deficiencies. Design consultation is a service unique to independent FIPS 140 consultants. Testing labs are not allowed to give product developers any guidance on how to rectify design deficiencies then test the module – that would be a conflict of interest.

Consultants are often called upon to develop the FIPS 140 validation-specific documentation such as the Security Policy and Finite State Model documents. They can also give product developers guidance on how to write the necessary vendor-provided documentation.

Testing Lab Costs

Cryptographic and security testing (CST) laboratories, like consultants can charge vendors on a T&M or on a fixed-price basis. Testing lab costs may vary depending on the experience level of the testers, the overhead costs of the testing lab, the testing lab's location, the complexity of the product, the number of products, and the security level of the validation. Table 10 gives some estimated testing lab costs for level 1 and 2 validation testing.

Security Level	Low Estimate	High Estimate
Level 1	$20,000	$35,000
Level 2	$30,000	$45,000

Table 10: Estimated Testing Lab Costs

Testing lab personnel may need to travel to the product developer site to gather more detailed information or to conduct specific tests, and/or review source code. Travel-associated costs will vary depending on the situation. The estimates shown in Table 10 do not include travel costs.

As mentioned in the Due Diligence section of this chapter, product developers should obtain competitive quotes from a number of accredited testing labs. Table 11 lists the 19 CMVP-approved FIPS 140 testing labs (as of October 2010). The NIST website maintains a current list of accredited labs [CSTL].

Laboratory Name	Location
AEGISOLVE, INC.	Paso Robles, CA USA
Aspect Labs	Santa Clara, CA USA
atsec information security corporation	Austin, TX USA
CEAL: a CygnaCom Solutions Laboratory	McLean, VA USA
COACT Inc. CAFE Laboratory	Columbia, MD USA
Computer Sciences Corporation	Hanover, MD USA
DOMUS IT Security Laboratory	Kanata, Ontario Canada
ECSEC Laboratory Inc.	Tokyo, Japan
Epoche & Espri	Madrid, Spain
EWA - Canada	Ottawa, Ontario Canada
ICSA Labs	Mechanicsburg, PA USA
InfoGard Laboratories, Inc.	San Luis Obispo, CA USA
Information Technology Security Center	Tokyo, Japan

SAIC Accredited Testing & Evaluation Labs	Columbia, MD USA
SAIC (Formerly Atlan)	McLean, VA USA
stratsec lab	Canberra, Australia
TTC IT Security Evaluation Laboratory	Banciao City, Taiwan
TÜV Informationstechnik GmbH	Essen, Germany
Underwriters Laboratories, Inc.	Northbrook, IL USA

Table 11: List of Accredited Testing Labs

Managing Project Scope

A key factor in driving the cost of the FIPS 140 validation is the scope of the cryptographic module itself and the security level being pursued. Chapter 8: Security Requirements will go into more detail about the FIPS 140 security requirements and levels, but it is important to assess the effort (and thus the cost) involved in the project. The goal of most product developers is to successfully complete the FIPS 140 validation while minimizing costs within time and resource constraints.

One dimension that determines the complexity and thus the cost of the FIPS 140 validation is the scope of the cryptographic boundary. The cryptographic boundary is the physical and logical border of the module under test. A larger boundary will typically require that more evidence be produced and more time from the lab to test the module. Both of these efforts are paid by the product developer. For example, a network router with virtual private network (VPN) capabilities could claim a cryptographic boundary that included the feature that encrypts internal configuration information. FIPS 140 validation of this feature may have no customer value and may be a good candidate for being excluded from the validation effort.

Another dimension to consider when assessing the scope of the FIPS 140 validation is the targeted security level. FIPS 140 provides for four increasingly stringent security levels against which modules may be validated. Higher security levels mean devoting more effort to preparing evidence documentation and more effort in testing the module. Customers may have set some expectations or requirements for the FIPS 140 validation security level, but increasing the security level of the validation may not yield an adequate return. Figure 15 illustrates the "diminishing returns" of higher security level validations.

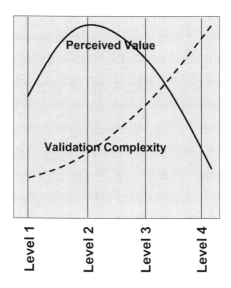

Figure 15: Value vs. Complexity

Chapter 14: Best Practices will discuss in more detail the need to manage customer expectations, but understanding and evaluating customer value is also important toward making sound business decisions regarding FIPS 140 validations.

NIST Fees

Cost recovery is a fee levied by NIST CMVP for the validation tasks and the program management responsibilities performed at NIST by the CMVP. The product developer is also responsible for paying these fees in order to complete the module validation. The fees vary by overall security level according to the following schedule that may also be found in the CMVP Management Manual [CMVP MM]:

Security Level	Cost Recovery Fee
Level 1	$2750
Level 2	$3750
Level 3	$5250
Level 4	$7250

Table 12: CMVP Fees

As illustrated in Table 12, the cost recovery fee amount varies depending on the security level of the validation. The higher the level, the greater the effort expended by CMVP, and thus the higher fee amount. This fee is assessed per certificate received. For example, if multiple appliances are included on one certificate, then only one cost recovery fee is assessed.

Timeline

Besides costs, timeliness is the next most important factor for product developers to consider regarding the FIPS 140 validation process. Understanding the process and timing for each phase is important to planning a successful validation project and setting expectations appropriately. The FIPS 140 validation process is comprised of three main phases:

1. Documentation
2. Testing
3. Validation

During the Documentation Phase, the module under test is thoroughly documented to address the FIPS 140 requirements along with supporting assurance documentation to support vendor claims. The publicly-disclosed Security Policy summaries the vendor security claims and how the FIPS 140 security requirements are met.

The Testing Phase begins when the documentation and module under test are submitted to an accredited FIPS 140 testing laboratory. The laboratory evaluates the documentation and tests the module. The documentation may need to be updated based on unresolved issues or comments from the testing laboratory.

Upon successful completion of testing, various documents are submitted to the CMVP to begin the Validation Phase. The CMVP will review the laboratory's test report and the module's Security Policy for accuracy and completeness. A successful review and validation lead to the issuing of a FIPS 140 validation certificate. The Validation Phase is composed of 4 sub-phases:

1. Review pending
2. Review
3. Coordination
4. Finalization

The module is in the Review Pending Phase while it waits in the queue for NIST CMVP resources to be freed up to conduct the actual review. The longest leg of the validation phase is waiting for NIST resources to begin the review. There is very little anyone can do to reduce this waiting time. There is no "jumping the queue" even with a Government customer request.

Once the Review Phase begins, the CMVP validator needs only a couple of weeks to review the Security Policy and the testing lab's report. The validator will highlight any questions and the module proceeds to the next phase.

The Coordination Phase consists of the evaluation lab addressing any questions the CMVP validator has. Responses to these questions might require involvement from the developer (or his/her consultant). There may be some exchange between CMVP and the testing lab, but typically, this phase is quick.

Once all of the validator questions have been addressed, the Finalization Phase begins with the assignment of a certificate number, printing and signing of the certificate. This, perhaps surprisingly, takes a couple of weeks as it requires signatures from both NIST as well as the Communications Security Establishment Canada (CSEC).

A product developer should typically plan for a validation to complete roughly in 7-13 months from the beginning of the Documentation Phase to the end of the Validation Phase. Table 13 illustrates a general estimated timeline for the validation effort.

Phase	Sub-Phase Duration	Phase Duration
Documentation		1 - 3 months
Testing		3 – 5 months
Validation		3 – 5 months
Review Pending	2 - 3 months	
Review	2 weeks	
Coordination	1 – 2 weeks	
Finalization	2 weeks	
Total		7 – 13 months

Table 13: Estimated Durations

There are obviously many dependencies that could dictate a shorter or longer validation process. For example, early identification and quick resolution of source code changes have a major effect on the schedule. The schedule for a FIPS 140 validation effort can also be compressed due to the quality and completeness of submission documentation. Clean, focused documentation reduces questions from and ramping time for the testing laboratory and provides a stronger baseline for testing.

Product developer response time to documentation updates and laboratory questions also impacts the overall schedule. As previously mentioned, high-quality submission deliverables will reduce the amount of rudimentary questions from the laboratory, but certainly questions/clarifications will arise at times. Quick turn-around helps reduce the time to complete the validation.

The CMVP validates each module before issuing a validation certificate. Given the proliferation of FIPS 140 submissions and the limited resources of the CMVP, the Validation Phase can take as long as 5 months. This time varies with the number of modules in the queue for review, whether or not the submission is a revalidation, and the completeness and accuracy of the documentation and testing. The module's validation security level will certainly have an effect on the project schedule. Higher levels of validation require increased effort for documentation and testing.

Summary

Time and money are critical considerations for any commercial product developer. FIPS 140 validation costs can be considerable and planning for those costs is an important business function. This chapter has provided information about the types of costs involved in the FIPS 140 validation as well as estimates for those costs.

The FIPS 140 validation process has several phases. Each phase has different activities and deliverables. Each party involved has a different role to play. Time and resource management is another important business planning function for the product developer. This chapter has given estimates for the amount of time that should be allocated for the different phases of the FIPS 140 validation.

Chapter 8: Security Requirements

The FIPS 140 standards [FIPS 140-2] describe the cryptographic module security requirements. Of course, it is important for the cryptographic module developer to understand these requirements; however, it is equally important for the developer to understand how the module will be tested during the FIPS 140 validation process. The FIPS 140 Derived Test Requirements [DTR] document describes the testing methods used by the Cryptographic Module Validation Program (CMVP)-accredited laboratories to validate whether cryptographic modules meet the FIPS 140 requirements. The Derived Test Requirements (DTR) contains detailed procedures the tester will execute to verify that the module and the associated documentation comply with the FIPS 140 requirements. These standardized methods are designed to provide objectivity and consistency during the testing process and across the different testing laboratories.

The DTR also details the requirements for vendor documentation that must be provided as evidence to demonstrate conformance. The cryptographic module must not only properly implement the security functions, the module and some of its characteristics must be adequately documented. The Security Policy document summarizes how the cryptographic module meets the FIPS 140 requirements while the vendor evidence documents provide the details necessary for the testing lab to conduct their in-depth validation. The Cryptographic and Security Testing (CST) lab will examine the documentation as well as the module during their evaluation.

The FIPS 140 security requirements are categorized into 11 sections. The requirements in each section are further categorized by security level. The CST lab will "rate" the cryptographic module in each section – giving them a security level. Table 14 summarizes the security requirements for levels 1 and 2 by section. Table 15 summarizes the security requirements for levels 3 and 4.

FIPS 140 Security Requirements		
Section	Level 1	Level 2
Cryptographic Module Specification	Specification of cryptographic module, cryptographic boundary, approved algorithms and approved modes of operation. Description of cryptographic module including all hardware, software and firmware components. Statement of module security policy.	
Cryptographic Module Ports and Interfaces	Required and optional interfaces. Specification of all interfaces and of all input and output ports.	
Roles, Services and Authentication	Logical separation for required and optional roles and services.	Role-based or identity-based operator authentication.
Finite State Model	Specification of finite state model. Required states and operational states. State transition diagram and specification of state transitions.	
Physical Security	Production grade equipment.	Locks or tamper evidence.
Operational Environments	Single operator. Executable code. Approved integrity technique.	Referenced PPs evaluated at EAL 2 with specified discretionary access control mechanisms and auditing.
Cryptographic Key Management	Key management mechanisms, random number generation, key establishment, key distribution, key input/output, key storage, and key zeroization.	
EMI/EMC	41 CFR FCC Part 15, Subpart B, Class A (business use). Applicable FCC requirements (for radio)	
Self-Tests	Power-up tests, cryptographic algorithm tests, software/firmware integrity tests, critical functions tests, conditional tests.	
Design Assurance	Configuration management (CM). Secure installation and generation, design and policy correspondence. Guidance documentation.	CM system. Secure distribution. Functional specification.
Mitigation of Other Attacks	Specification of mitigation of other attacks for which no testable requirements are currently available.	

Table 14: Security Requirements for Levels 1 & 2

FIPS 140 Security Requirements		
Section	Level 3	Level 4
Cryptographic Module Specification	Indicate when approved mode is selected.	
Cryptographic Module Ports and Interfaces	Date ports for unprotected CSP are logically or physically separated from all other data ports.	
Roles, Services and Authentication	Identity-based operator authentication.	
Finite State Model	Specification of finite state model. Required states and operational states. State transition diagram and specification of state transitions.	
Physical Security	Tamper detection and response to doors and covers.	Tamper detection and response envelope. EFP or EFT.
Operational Environments	Referenced PPs plus trusted path evaluated at EAL 3 plus security policy modeling.	Referenced PPs plus trusted path evaluated at EAL 4.
Cryptographic Key Management	Key management mechanisms, random number generation, key establishment, key distribution, key input/output, key storage, and key zeroization.	
EMI/EMC	41 CFR FCC Part 15, Subpart B, Class B (home use)	
Self-Tests	Power-up tests, cryptographic algorithm tests, software/firmware integrity tests, critical functions tests, conditional tests.	
Design Assurance	High-level language implementation.	Formal model. Detailed explanations. (Informal proofs). Pre-conditions and post-conditions.
Mitigation of Other Attacks	Specification of mitigation of other attacks for which no testable requirements are currently available.	

Table 15: Security Requirements for Levels 3 & 4

Security Levels

For each security requirement, the DTR describes the vendor documentation and tester instructions for each security level. That is, each security requirement described in the DTR has specific instructions to test for compliance at security levels 1, 2, 3 and 4:

- Security Level 1 – Basic security requirements
- Security Level 2 – Tamper evidence
- Security Level 3 – Intrusion prevention
- Security Level 4 – Complete envelope of protection

Security level 1 requirements are the least stringent, and security level 4 requirements are the most stringent. Modules are tested and rated to a security level for each section and also receive an overall security level, which is the lowest rating in all applicable sections. For example, a module may be validated at level 3 in 10 of the 11 sections, but if one section, for example, Physical Security, was validated at level 2 the module's overall level would be level 2.

Levels – Rules of Thumb

Level 1 is appropriate for software-only products because there are no physical security requirements.

Level 2 would be applicable to software products tested on specific hardware platforms in specific configurations or security appliances such as VPN routers.

Level 3, because of the physical tamper-evidence requirements, can only be met by purpose-built hardware products. The hardware may house software and firmware, but the hardware must support the physical security requirements.

Level 4 requires purpose-built hardware with stringent physical security protection designed with formal development methods.

The decision to pursue a specific level is governed by several factors. The first factor for choosing a validation level is customer/end user requirements. Most end users do not have requirements further than "FIPS 140 validation." Some agencies have specific requirements for an overall validation level (either by technology type or across the board), though this is not common.

A second factor for deciding which level to pursue arises from the competitive landscape. If the majority of competitors are validated at level 2, then a benchmark has been set. In this situation, a level 1 validation may not be practical; however, a level 3 validation could provide competitive advantage.

Product design also plays a role in deciding which validation level to pursue; product features or capabilities may prohibit testing at higher levels. For example, if the module does not support identity-based authentication, then it cannot be tested at level 3 for Roles, Services, and Authentication (and subsequently cannot achieve overall level 3).

Security Requirements

The requirements for FIPS 140 validation are categorized, tested and rated in the following 11 sections:

1. Cryptographic Module Specification
2. Cryptographic Module Ports and Interfaces
3. Roles, Services, and Authentication
4. Finite State Model
5. Physical Security
6. Operational Environment
7. Cryptographic Key Management
8. Electro-Magnetic Interference/Compatibility (EMI/EMC)
9. Self-Tests
10. Design Assurance
11. Mitigation of Other Attacks

Some of these sections may not be applicable to particular modules under test. For example, a purpose-built appliance with a proprietary, non-modifiable operating system would likely not be subject to the requirements in the Operational Environment section. Similarly, if the module does not claim to mitigate other attacks, then the Mitigation of Other Attacks section is not applicable.

Some of the requirements are tested by examining the cryptographic module documentation. Other requirements are tested by examining the module implementation itself. Documentation requirements are discussed later in this chapter. The following sections describe the module implementation requirements.

Cryptographic Module Specification

A cryptographic module is defined as a set of hardware, software, and/or firmware that implements cryptographic functions such as encrypt, decrypt, and key generation. The cryptographic module must implement at least one FIPS 140-approved security function. The FIPS

140-approved security functions can be found in FIPS 140 Annex A [FIPS 140-2 A] and were discussed in Chapter 5 as:

1. Symmetric key
2. Asymmetric key
3. Message authentication
4. Random number generation
5. Secure hash
6. Key management

The cryptographic module must be contained entirely within the defined cryptographic boundary. The cryptographic boundary is an explicitly-defined physical perimeter for the cryptographic module. The boundary must contain any hardware components that store or protect any software or firmware components of the cryptographic module. For example, a virtual private network (VPN) appliance product will be the hardware enclosure or case for the product including any access panels, doors or ventilation slots.

Figure 16 summarizes the security requirements for the cryptographic module specifications for each security level. The # column indicates the reference number used in the FIPS 140 Derived Test Requirements (DTR) document for the security requirement. The "X" in the boxes indicate that the requirement applies to the given security level. The bold-faced "**X**" indicates that this is a new requirement for that level over the lower levels.

Since the cryptographic module specification is a document, most of the security requirements for this section are explained in the Document Requirements section of this chapter. The cryptographic module functions, cryptographic boundary and all of the module components will be described in the cryptographic module specification.

	#	1	2	3	4	Short Description
		Security Level				
		1	**2**	**3**	**4**	
Cryptographic Module Specifications	1	X	X	X	X	Implements crypto within boundary
	2	X	X	X	X	Implements at least one security function
	3	X	X	X	X	Describe Approved Mode of operation
	4			X	X	Indicate when Approved Mode is selected
	5	X	X	X	X	Boundary is an explicitly-defined physical perimeter
	6	X	X	X	X	Includes hardware processor with software
	7	X	X	X	X	Documentation requirements
	8	X	X	X	X	Document components, boundary & configuration
	9	X	X	X	X	Document and explain excluded components
	10	X	X	X	X	Document ports and interfaces
	11	X	X	X	X	Document controls and status
	12	X	X	X	X	List all security functions
	13	X	X	X	X	Include hardware block diagram
	14	X	X	X	X	Document the design
	15	X	X	X	X	Document all security information
	16	X	X	X	X	Document the security policy

Figure 16: Cryptographic Module Specifications

Cryptographic Module Ports and Interfaces

Cryptographic modules must limit all physical access to physical ports and limit all information flow to logical interfaces. Module interfaces are logically distinct from each other. A cryptographic module shall define the following four logical interfaces:

1. Data Input Interface
2. Data Output Interface
3. Control Input Interface
4. Status Output Interface

Data and control inputs will be distinct from data and status outputs. All input data must enter the module through the data input interface along the input data path. Similarly, all output data exiting the cryptographic module through the data output interface will exit only through the output data path. Output access will be further restricted when key information is being handled by the cryptographic module. Figure 17 summarizes the security requirements for the cryptographic module ports and interfaces.

Physical ports may be physical connections such as Ethernet ports or wireless radio ports. Physical ports are mapped to logical input and/or output interfaces. The Ethernet port, for example, can serve as both a logical input as well as a logical output interface.

	#	Security Level				Short Description
		1	2	3	4	
Ports and Interfaces	1	X	X	X	X	Restrict information flow to ports and interfaces
	2	X	X	X	X	Logically distinct interfaces
	3	X	X	X	X	Data I/O, control, status interfaces
	4	X	X	X	X	All data input enters data input interface
	5	X	X	X	X	All data output exits data output interface
	6	X	X	X	X	Inhibit data output on error and self-test
	7	X	X	X	X	All control input through control input interface
	8	X	X	X	X	All status output exit through status output interface
	9	X	X	X	X	All external power is via power port
	10	X	X	X	X	Distinguish between data, control, status
	11	X	X	X	X	All input data pass through data input path
	12	X	X	X	X	All output data pass through data output path
	13	X	X	X	X	Output data path disconnected for key handling
	14	X	X	X	X	Two actions required to output data
	15	X	X	X	X	Document ports, interfaces, data paths
	16			X	X	Physically separate ports for plaintext
	17			X	X	Logically separate interfaces for plaintext
	18			X	X	Input plaintext directly

Figure 17: Ports and Interfaces

The module implementation must reflect these input and output interfaces and data paths. The associated documentation will describe these interfaces and ports for the tester. This documentation will be further explained in the Document Requirements section of this chapter.

Roles, Services, and Authentication

The cryptographic module will support roles and their corresponding services for authorized operators. Authentication mechanisms are used to authenticate an operator accessing the module and to verify that the operator is authorized to assume the role and perform the services within that role.

Roles and Services

Figure 18 illustrates the requirements for roles and services of the cryptographic module. The cryptographic module must support the following operator roles:

- User Role
- Crypto Officer Role
- Maintenance Role, if maintenance services are provided

The User Role is authorized to perform general security operational functions. The Crypto Officer Role can perform cryptographic initialization and management functions. The Maintenance Role performs maintenance functions on the cryptographic module such as diagnostics.

Documentation will provide the details of what services are performed by which roles. Details for this documentation will be described in the Document Requirements section of this chapter. The documentation will reflect how the cryptographic module will provide the following services to operators depending upon their roles:

- Show Status
- Perform Self-Tests
- Performed Approved Security Function
- Optional: Bypass Function

	#	Security Level				Short Description
		1	2	3	4	
Roles and Services	1	X	X	X	X	Support authorized roles and services
	2	X	X	X	X	Maintain separation of roles
	3	X	X	X	X	Support user and crypto officer roles
	4	X	X	X	X	Support maintenance role
	5	X	X	X	X	Zeroize plaintext on enter/exit maintenance role
	6	X	X	X	X	Document all authorized roles
	7	X	X	X	X	Services refer to all services, operations & functions
	8	X	X	X	X	Service inputs are all data for services
	9	X	X	X	X	Service outputs are all data from services
	10	X	X	X	X	Each service input results in service output
	11	X	X	X	X	Performs status, self-test & security functions
	12	X	X	X	X	Two actions required to bypass
	13	X	X	X	X	Show bypass status
	14	X	X	X	X	Documents all services, inputs and outputs

Figure 18: Roles and Services

Authentication

Authentication mechanisms verify that operators requesting access to the cryptographic module have permission to assume the requested role and perform the services within that role. Figure 19 lists the

99

authentication requirement for each of the security levels. Depending on the security level, the cryptographic module will support the following authentication mechanisms:

- Role-Based Authentication
- Identity-Based Authentication

	#	Security Level 1	2	3	4	Short Description
Authentication	15	X	X	X	X	Specify services w/o authorized role
	16	X	X	X	X	Operator authorization types
	17		X			Role-based authentication
	18		X			Authenticate role change
	19			X	X	Individual identity-based authentication
	20			X	X	Authenticate individual role change
	21	X	X	X	X	Re-authenticate on power up
	22		X	X	X	Protect authentication data
	23	X	X	X	X	Use default authorization data on initial access
	24		X	X	X	Strength of authorization
	25		X	X	X	Random authentication less than 1:1M
	26		X	X	X	Random authentication less than 1:100K in 1 min.
	27		X	X	X	Obscure authentication feedback
	28		X	X	X	Feedback does not weaken authentication strength
	29	X	X	X	X	Document authentication details
	30	X				Require role if no authentication
	31		X			Role-based authentication to control module
	32			X	X	Identity-based authentication to control module

Figure 19: Authentication

At security level 2, if role-based authentication is supported, operators will be required to assume a role (e.g., "User" or "Admin") and be authenticated against it in order to operate the module. Identity-based authentication is considered more secure and is required at security levels 3 and 4. For security level 2 and above, authentication mechanisms meet strength requirements by demonstrating:

- Probablility of access by random guess is 1:1,000,000
- Probablity of access using multiple random guess attempts in one minute is 1:100,000
- Authentication data will be visually obscured during authentication
- Feedback to operators will not weaken the authentication mechanism

Finite State Model

Figure 20 summarizes the requirements for the finite state model. The finite state model is a document describing the module states and transitions and is described in the Documentation Requirements section of this chapter. The cryptographic module must include and be described using the following operational and error states:

- Power On and Off States
- Crypto Officer States
- Key and Critical Security Parameter (CSP) Entry States
- User States
- Self-Test States
- Error States

	#	Security Level 1	2	3	4	Short Description
Finite State Model	1	X	X	X	X	Specify operation using finite state transition model
	2	X	X	X	X	Operation and error states
	3	X	X	X	X	Recovery from error states
	4	X	X	X	X	Maintenance state with maintenance role
	5	X	X	X	X	Document state transitions and I/O events

Figure 20: Finite State Model

Optionally, the cryptographic module may include the following states if the capabilities are provided by the module:

- Bypass States
- Maintenance States

The finite state model requirements are primarily fulfilled by documenting the states within the cryptographic module, so the details of the FIPS 140 security requirements are described in the Documentation Requirements section of this chapter.

Physical Security

The cryptographic module is required to provide physical security mechanisms to restrict unauthorized access to the module. Physical security requirements are categorized into general physical security

101

requirements and requirements unique to three physical configurations (embodiments) that are defined by FIPS 140. The physical security requirement categories are:

- General Requirements
- Single-Chip
- Multi-Chip Embedded
- Multi-Chip Standalone

Tables 16 and 17 below summarize the general physical security requirements and the requirements for all supported configurations.

Regardless of the security level and configuration (embodiment), the cryptographic module will use production-grade components with protection from environmental or other physical damage.

If a maintenance role is provided, physical access will be through the defined maintenance access interface including any doors or covers. The maintenance access interface will be protected with appropriate security mechanisms. For example, in order to perform a diagnostic function the maintenance operator must open a door on the module's case; the door must use at least tamper-evident seals.

Level	General Requirements	Single-Chip
1	Use production-grade components.	No additional requirements.
2	Tamper evidence.	Opaque tamper-evident coating on chip or enclosure
3	Automatic zeroization with maintenance access. Tamper response and zeroization. Protected vents.	Hard opaque tamper-evident coating on chip or strong removal-resistant and penetration resistant enclosure.
4	EFP or EFT for temperature and voltage.	Hard opaque removal-resistant coating on chip.

Table 16: Physical Security Requirements

Level	Multiple-Chip Embedded	Multiple-Chip Standalone
1	Use production-grade enclosure or removable covers.	Use production-grade enclosure.
2	Opaque tamper-evident encapsulating material or enclosure with tamper-evident seals or pick-resistant locks for doors or removable covers.	Opaque enclosure with tamper-evident seals or pick-resistant locks for doors or removable covers.
3	Hard opaque potting material encapsulation of multiple chip circuitry embodiments.	Hard opaque potting material encapsulation of multiple chip circuitry embodiment or strong enclosure with access attempts causing serious damage.
4	Tamper detection envelope with tamper response and zeroization circuitry.	Tamper detection/ response envelope with tamper response.

Table 17: Physical Security Requirements (cont.)

Figure 21 provides a summary of the general physical security requirements for all security levels. At level 2 and above, the cryptographic module will provide opaque, tamper-evident seals or coatings. For level 3 and above, the coatings and seals will be hard, opaque and tamper-resistant; meaning any attempt to remove or penetrate the coatings will result in damage to the module. Also, all plaintext security information will be zeroized upon access through the maintenance interface.

General Requirements

		Security Level				
	#	1	2	3	4	Short Description
Physical Security - General	1	X	X	X	X	Physical restrictions to restrict access
	2	X	X	X	X	All components are protected
	3	X	X	X	X	All physical embodiments
	4	X	X	X	X	Specify physical embodiment and security level
	5	X	X	X	X	Specify physical security mechanisms used
	6	X	X	X	X	Maintenance access interface for maintenance role
	7	X	X	X	X	Physical access paths for maintenance access
	8	X	X	X	X	Safeguard removable covers for maintenance access
	9	X	X	X	X	Zeroize plaintext for maintenance
	10	X	X	X	X	Document maintenance access interface
	11	X				Security level 1 requirements
	12	X	X	X	X	Production grade components
	13	X	X	X	X	Zeroize plaintext for maintenance
	14	X	X	X	X	Periodic zeroization
	15		X	X	X	Security level 2 requirements
	16		X	X	X	Tamper evidence
	17			X	X	Security level 3 requirements
	18			X	X	Doors have tamper response & zeroization
	19			X	X	Zeroize when cover removed
	20			X	X	Tamper response & zeroization remain operational
	21			X	X	Ventilation holes prevent probing
	22				X	Security level 4 requirements
	23				X	Include environmental failure protection

Figure 21: Physical Security - General

For security levels 3 and 4, Physical Security requirement #21 states that if the cryptographic module contains ventilation holes or slits then physical probing will be prevented by a 90 degree bend or obstruction made of a substantial blocking material. For appliance products that have ventilation slits, this means the appliance case must block the view into the interior of the enclosure and prevent physical probing.

Some appliance vendors have had to go to special efforts to satisfy the interpretation of this requirement. The apparent threat this requirement addresses is the idea that an attacker could look inside the enclosure to identify the integrated circuits (IC) used and from there be able to attack the module. This requirement also attempts to address the threat that an attacker could insert an electronic probe to measure the signals across the circuits and be able to infiltrate the module.

Single-Chip

The single-chip embodiment is defined as a cryptographic module that is completely contained within a single integrated circuit (IC) or chip. The IC may be used as a standalone module or may be embedded or integrated into a larger module. An example of a single-chip cryptographic module is a smart card. Figure 22 illustrates the physical security requirements for a single-chip embodiment.

		Security Level				
	#	1	2	3	4	Short Description
Physical Security - Single Chip	24		X	X	X	Single chip security level 2
	25		X	X	X	Covered with tamper evident coating
	26		X	X	X	Covered with opaque tamper evident coating
	27			X	X	Single chip level 3
	28			X	X	Hard opaque tamper evident coating
	29			X	X	Module damage upon enclosure tampering
	30				X	Single chip level 4
	31				X	Hard opaque tamper resistant coating
	32				X	Solvency characteristics of tamper-resistant coating

Figure 22: Physical Security - Single-Chip

Security requirements specific to single-chip cryptographic modules begin at security level 2 and start with tamper-evident coatings. At security levels 3 and 4, the single-chip module must be coated with hard, opaque coatings such that the module would be significantly damaged should an attacker attempt to tamper with the device.

Multi-Chip Embedded

Multi-chip embedded cryptographic modules are defined as two or more interconnected ICs within a protected enclosure. Printed circuit boards that may be installed as an adapter or expansion board can be considered a multi-chip embedded module.

Figure 23 lists brief descriptions of the physical security requirements unique to multi-chip embedded cryptographic modules. Security levels 2 and 3 focus on tamper-evidence mechanisms including coatings and locked doors and covers.

	#	Security Level				Short Description
		1	2	3	4	
Physical Security - Multi-Chip Embedded	33	X	X	X	X	Multi-chip embedded level 1 requirements
	34	X	X	X	X	Production grade enclosure used
	35		X	X	X	Multi-chip embedded level 2 requirements
	36		X	X	X	Tamper evident coating or enclosure
	37		X	X	X	Enclosure doors and covers secured with locks
	38			X	X	Multi-chip embedded level 3 requirements
	39			X	X	Opaque, hard coating on circuitry
	40				X	Multi-chip embedded level 4 requirements
	41				X	Tamper detection envelope
	42				X	Tamper response and zeroization
	43				X	Tamper response continuous monitoring
	44				X	Zeroize upon tamper detection
	45				X	Tamper response operational with plaintext

Figure 23: Physical Security - Multi-Chip Embedded

At level 4, multi-chip embedded modules must also provide continuously monitoring tamper response and zeroization circuitry so that all plaintext keys and critical security parameters (CSP) will be zeroized upon detection of tampering.

Multi-Chip Standalone

Multi-chip standalone cryptographic modules are two or more interconnected ICs contained within a protective enclosure. Software modules are considered multi-chip modules with respect to FIPS 140 physical security requirements because the software is tested and validated on a given set of computer hardware platforms that will provide the physical security. Other examples of multi-chip standalone modules are routers and other appliances.

Figure 24 summarizes the physical security requirements specific to multi-chip standalone embodiments. These requirements are similar to the physical security requirements for multi-chip embedded modules.

	#	Security Level				Short Description
		1	2	3	4	
Physical Security - Multi-Chip Standalone	46	X	X	X	X	Multi-chip standalone level 1
	47	X	X	X	X	Use metal or hard plastic enclosure
	48		X	X	X	Multi-chip standalone level 2
	49		X	X	X	Use opaque enclosure
	50		X	X	X	Tamper-evident locked doors and covers
	51			X	X	Multi-chip standalone level 3
	52			X	X	Opaque, hard epoxy covers circuitry
	53			X	X	Use strong enclosure
	54				X	Multi-chip standalone level 4
	55				X	Tamper detection envelope around enclosure
	56				X	Detect cutting and drilling
	57				X	Include tamper response and zeroization circuitry
	58				X	Tamper response continuous monitoring
	59				X	Tamper response operational with plaintext

Figure 24: Physical Security - Multi-Chip Standalone

Environmental Failure Protection/Test

Physical security requirements at level 4 include environmental failure protection (EFP) or environmental failure test (EFT). The two alternative requirements are summarized in Figure 25. EFP mechanisms protect the cryptographic module from physical environmental threats such as excessive temperature or voltage. The module can meet the FIPS 140 security requirements by either providing EFP from excessive temperature and voltage, or undergo EFT to demonstrate that the security of the module will not be compromised under extreme environmental conditions.

	#	Security Level				Short Description
		1	2	3	4	
Physical Security - EFP/EFT	60				X	Environmental failure protection or test
	61				X	Protect against unusual environments (Alternative 1)
	62				X	Respond to temperature and voltage fluctuations
	63				X	Continuously monitor temperature and voltage
	64				X	Shutdown or zeroize outside temp or voltage ranges
	65				X	Document normal operating ranges
	66				X	Environmental failure testing (Alternative 2)
	67				X	Demonstrate failure protection
	68				X	Temperature range testing
	69				X	Document environment testing

Figure 25: EFP/EFT

107

Operational Environment

There are basically three types of operational environments: general-purpose, modifiable and limited. Operational environment security requirements deal with the modifiable or general-purpose operating systems underlying the cryptographic module. Products such as smart cards and appliances may not need to meet the operational environment requirements because the underlying operating environments are considered to be limited or non-modifiable. However, products such as application software will have to meet these requirements because application software generally will be executing on top of general-purpose operating systems. These platform operating systems will need to meet the operating system requirements summarized in Figure 26.

	#	Security Level 1	2	3	4	Short Description
	1	X	X	X	X	Operating system requirements
	2	X	X	X	X	Document operational environment
	3	X	X	X	X	OS level 1 requirements
	4	X				Single operator mode only
	5	X				Restrict key access
	6	X				No interrupts
	7	X	X	X	X	Secure installation
	8	X	X	X	X	Use approved integrity technique
	9		X			Security level 2 requirements
	10		X			Control by OS with CC EAL 2
Operational Environment	11		X	X	X	OS DAC specifies execute controls
	12		X	X	X	OS DAC specifies modify controls
	13		X	X	X	OS DAC specifies read controls
	14		X	X	X	OS DAC specifies enter controls
	15		X	X	X	OS prevents modifications
	16		X	X	X	OS prevents reading
	17		X	X	X	OS provides audit
	18		X	X	X	Audit crypto officer events
	19		X	X	X	Audit other events
	20			X		Security level 3 requirements
	21			X		Control by OS with CC EAL 3 and PP
	22			X	X	Use trusted communications for security info
	23			X	X	Use trusted path for TSF to operator communication
	24			X	X	Trusted path activated by TSF operator
	25			X	X	Audit trusted path events
	26				X	Security level 4 requirements
	27				X	Control by OS with CC EAL 4 and PP

Figure 26: Operational Environment

For those modules executing on general-purpose operating systems or otherwise modifiable operational environments, the operating system requirements must be met. The operating system requirements are intended to increase the protection of the cryptographic keys, critical security parameters (CSP), and software components as the security level increases. Operating systems are also required to be evaluated using the Common Criteria [CC] evaluation standards and approved Protection Profiles [FIPS 140-2 B].

Cryptographic Key Management

Cryptographic key management requirements cover the entire key lifecycle from creation to elimination and are intended to protect keys and critical security parameters (CSP) from unauthorized access or modification.

General Requirements and Random Number Generators

The general requirements for key management for all levels protect against the unauthorized modification or substitution of all keys (public, private and secret). In addition, secret and private keys are protected against unauthorized disclosure.

Random number generators (RNG) are required to use approved random number generator algorithms [FIPS 140-2 C] and must pass the applicable tests.

| | # | Security Level | | | | Short Description |
		1	2	3	4	
Key Mgmt. - General & RNG	1	X	X	X	X	Protect secret, private keys
	2	X	X	X	X	Protect public keys
	3	X	X	X	X	Document all keys
	4	X	X	X	X	Pass continuous RNG test
	5					No description
	6	X	X	X	X	Subject to RNG algorithm test
	7	X	X	X	X	Nondeterministic RNG comply with requirements
	8	X	X	X	X	Use approved RNG for key generation
	9	X	X	X	X	Seed and seed key not the same value
	10	X	X	X	X	Document all RNGs

Figure 27: General & RNG

Figure 27 gives a brief description of the general key management and random number generator requirements. Documentation will

109

provide testers more details for key management. The documentation requirements will be described in the Document Requirements section at the end of this chapter.

Key Generation and Establishment

Cryptographic modules that generate keys internally must use approved key generation methods. Contrary to statements within the FIPS 140-2 standard document [FIPS 140-2], the approved key generation methods are not documented in FIPS 140 Annex C [FIPS 140-2 C]. Instead, the approved key generation methods are documented in the FIPS 140 Implementation Guidance document [IG]. Figure 28 summarizes the key establishment requirements for all security levels.

Key establishment is defined as the method used to distribute keys securely by manual and/or automated means. FIPS 140-approved key establishment methods are described in FIPS 140 Annex D [FIPS 140-2 D]. The approved methods for key establishment for symmetric (private) keys are documented in FIPS 140 Implementation Guidance [IG] Section 7.1. NIST Special Publications 800-56A [SP 800-56A] and 800-56B [SP 800-56B] document the approved methods for establishing asymmetric (public) keys.

	#	1	2	3	4	Short Description
		Security Level				
Key Mgmt. - Key Gen & Estab.	11	X	X	X	X	Use approved key generation
	12	X	X	X	X	Use approved RNG for key generation
	13	X	X	X	X	Guessing seed value equals guessing key value
	14	X	X	X	X	Seed key meets key entry requirements
	15	X	X	X	X	Secure intermediate key generation values
	16	X	X	X	X	Document all key generation methods
	17	X	X	X	X	Use only approved key establishment
	18	X	X	X	X	OTAR uses approved standards
	19	X	X	X	X	Guessing key method equals guessing key value
	20	X	X	X	X	Key transport meets requirements
	21	X	X	X	X	Document key establishment methods

Figure 28: Key Generation & Establishment

A radio communications cryptographic module may implement Over-The-Air-Rekeying (OTAR) in place of a key establishment method. The OTAR method used will follow the TIA/EIA Telecommunications Systems Bulletin, APCO Project 25, Digital Over-The-Air-Rekeying Protocol [OTAR]. The OTAR standard defines the messages and procedures for providing OTAR and related key management services.

110

The standard includes methods of encrypting and sending encryption keys and other related key management messages through the common air interface (CAI) in a way that protects them from disclosure and unauthorized modification.

Key Entry and Output

Cryptographic and seed keys can be entered or output manually through an interface such as a keypad. At security levels 1 and 2, keys established using manual methods may be input or output in plaintext form. At security levels 3 and 4, manually-established keys must be entered in encrypted form or use an approved split-knowledge technique requiring operator authentication. Figure 29 illustrates the key entry and output requirements for all security levels.

	#	Security Level				Short Description
		1	2	3	4	
Key Mgmt. - Entry & Output	22	X	X	X	X	Key I/O done manually or electronically
	23	X	X	X	X	Seed key entry same as key entry
	24	X	X	X	X	Encrypted keys use approved algorithms
	25	X	X	X	X	Associate key to correct entity
	26	X	X	X	X	Verify manually entered keys
	27	X	X	X	X	No plaintext key display
	28	X	X	X	X	Document key entry and output
	29	X	X	X	X	Encrypt secret and private keys
	30			X	X	Encrypt secret and private keys
	31			X	X	Securely output secret and private keys
	32			X	X	Separate authentication with split knowledge
	33			X	X	Enter plaintext key directly
	34			X	X	Two key components with split knowledge
	35			X	X	Document proof split knowledge
	36			X	X	Split knowledge procedures

Figure 29: Key Entry and Output

Automatically-established keys for all security levels are to be entered or output electronically via smart cards or other devices in encrypted form.

Key Storage and Zeroization

Plaintext secret and private keys stored within the cryptographic module shall not be accessible from outside the cryptographic module to unauthorized operators. The cryptographic module must associate all cryptographic keys with the correct assigned entity.

Cryptographic modules will be able to zeroize all of its plaintext secret and private cryptographic keys and critical security parameters (CSP). Zeroizing keys and other CSPs destroys the keys and ends the key lifecycle.

Figure 30 summarizes the key storage and zeroization requirements for all security levels. Key storage and zeroization methods will be documented and reviewed by the testing lab. Documentation requirements will be described in more detail in the Document Requirements section of this chapter.

		Security Level				
	#	1	2	3	4	Short Description
Key Mgmt. - Storage & Zero.	37	X	X	X	X	Key stored in plaintext or encrypted
	38	X	X	X	X	Plaintext keys not accessible externally
	39	X	X	X	X	Associate keys to proper entity
	40	X	X	X	X	Document key storage methods
	41	X	X	X	X	Provide method to zeroize keys
	42	X	X	X	X	Document zeroization methods

Figure 30: Key Storage and Zeroization

Electro-Magnetic Interference/Compatibility (EMI/EMC)

FIPS 140 includes electro-magnetic interference and electro-magnetic compatibility (EMI/EMC) requirements for unintentional radiators because this type of radiation may give attackers insight into the operation of the cryptographic module, thus potentially compromising security. The Federal Communications Commission (FCC) standards used place limits on the radiated emissions of the module in order to be in conformance with the standard.

To meet the security requirements for electro-magnetic interference (EMI) and electro-magnetic compatibility (EMC) for security levels 1 and 2, the cryptographic module must meet the EMI/EMC requirements specified in 47 Code of Federal Regulations, Part 15, Subpart B, Unintentional Radiators, Digital Devices, Class A [FCC]. For levels 3 and 4, Class B requirements must be met. Figure 31 illustrates the EMI/EMC requirements in table form.

| | # | Security Level | | | | Short Description |
		1	2	3	4	
EMI/EMC	1	X	X	X	X	Meet EMI/EMC requirements
	2	X	X	X	X	Radios meet FCC requirements
	3	X	X	X	X	Document EMI/EMC conformance
	4	X	X			Conform to 47 Code of Federal Regs Class A
	5			X	X	Conform to 47 Code of Federal Regs Class B

Figure 31: EMI/EMC

Self-Tests

There are two types of self-tests the cryptographic module must support: power-up self-tests and conditional self-tests. These self-tests help ensure that the cryptographic module is operating correctly. If any of these self-tests fail, the cryptographic module will enter an error state, an error status will be output, and the module will not perform any cryptographic functions.

Power-Up Self-Tests

Power-up self-tests shall be executed on module power-up or on demand by an authorized operator. A known-answer algorithm test will be performed on power-up for all of the supported cryptographic functions including random number generation, encryption, decryption and authentication. Software/firmware integrity tests will be performed using an error detection code (EDC) or authentication technique at power-up. Finally, a critical function test will be performed at power-up for all functions supporting the secure operations of the cryptographic module.

Figure 32 summarizes the general self-test requirements along with the power-up self-test requirements. Note that all of the security requirements for power-up self-tests are the same across all security levels; as a result, the security level claimed for this category will be the same as the overall security level for the cryptographic module.

	#	1	2	3	4	Short Description
		Security Level				
	#	**1**	**2**	**3**	**4**	**Short Description**
Self-Test - General & Power-Up	1	X	X	X	X	Perform power-up and continuous self-tests
	2	X	X	X	X	Power-up self-test on power-up
	3	X	X	X	X	Conditional self-test on security function initiation
	4	X	X	X	X	Enter error state on self-test failure
	5	X	X	X	X	No operation in error state
	6	X	X	X	X	No output in error state
	7	X	X	X	X	Document self-tests, errors & conditions
	8	X	X	X	X	Perform power-up tests
	9	X	X	X	X	Automatic power-up test
	10	X	X	X	X	Test output to status output
	11	X	X	X	X	Inhibit output during tests
	12	X	X	X	X	Allow manual power-up test
	13	X	X	X	X	power-up algorithm, integrity & critical function tests
	14					No description
	15					No description
	16	X	X	X	X	Known answer algorithm tests on all functions
	17	X	X	X	X	Fail on wrong answer
	18	X	X	X	X	Use pair-wise consistency tests
	19	X	X	X	X	Test message digest algorithms
	20	X	X	X	X	Test independent implementations
	21	X	X	X	X	Fail on differing results between implementations
	22	X	X	X	X	Use error detection code to validate SW
	23	X	X	X	X	Fail EDC test on no match
	24	X	X	X	X	EDC test must be 16 bit length
	25	X	X	X	X	Other critical function test on power-up
	26	X	X	X	X	Test other conditions with conditional tests
	27	X	X	X	X	Document all critical functions
	28					No description

Figure 32: Self-Tests - General & Power-Up

Conditional Self-Tests

If the cryptographic module performs certain functions or has specific capabilities, conditional tests must be performed to demonstrate that the module functions are performing correctly. Figure 33 summarizes the conditional self-test requirements for all security levels. Note that all of the security requirements for conditional self-tests are the same across all security levels; as a result, the security level claimed for this category will be the same as the overall security level for the cryptographic module.

Pair-wise encryption/decryption tests will be performed if the module uses public or private keys. Load tests using an approved authentication mechanism must be performed should the module include software or firmware that can be externally loaded. A test for

114

the required 16-bit error detection code (EDC) will be executed if the module uses keys that can be manually entered. If a random number generator is used within the module, a continuous random number generation test will be run. Any bypass capability will be tested to check the correct switching from normal cryptographic operation to bypass mode.

	#	Security Level				Short Description
		1	2	3	4	
Self-Tests - Conditional	29	X	X	X	X	Perform conditional tests
	30	X	X	X	X	Perform pair-wise consistency tests
	31	X	X	X	X	Test key transport method
	32					No description
	33	X	X	X	X	Test key consistency for digital signature
	34	X	X	X	X	Perform software load test
	35	X	X	X	X	Authentication software at load time
	36	X	X	X	X	SW integrity test fail when result does not match
	37	X	X	X	X	Test manual key entry
	38	X	X	X	X	Apply EDC on keys using duplicate entries
	39	X	X	X	X	EDC test must be 16 bit length
	40	X	X	X	X	Fail if EDC cannot be verified
	41	X	X	X	X	Perform continuous RNG tests
	42	X	X	X	X	Test RNG-generated n-bit blocks
	43	X	X	X	X	RNG less than 16 bits
	44	X	X	X	X	Test bypass capabilities
	45	X	X	X	X	Test for correct bypass operation on switch
	46	X	X	X	X	Test automatic bypass
	47	X	X	X	X	No single point of failure
	48	X	X	X	X	Document switching mechanism

Figure 33: Self-Tests - Conditional

Design Assurance

Design assurance is the set of security practices employed during module design, development, deployment, and operation. Figure 34 depicts a summary of the design assurance requirements. The design assurance security requirements include the use of a configuration management (CM) system for the cryptographic module, all of its components, and the FIPS 140-associated documentation. Configuration management systems control and monitor the access and modification of the CM contents and limit access to only authorized entities.

115

	#	Security Level				Short Description
		1	2	3	4	
Design Assurance	1	X	X	X	X	Implement configuration management
	2	X	X	X	X	Use unique identifiers for each configuration item
	3	X	X	X	X	Document secure installation setup
	4		X	X	X	Document secure distribution and delivery
	5	X	X	X	X	Security level 1 requirements
	6	X	X	X	X	Document design and security policy
	7	X	X	X	X	Document source code for components
	8	X	X	X	X	Document includes hardware schematics
	9		X	X	X	Security level 2 requirements
	10		X	X	X	Documentation includes functional specification
	11			X	X	Security level 3 requirements
	12			X	X	Use high level language implementation
	13			X	X	Hardware uses high level specification language
	14				X	Security level 4 requirements
	15				X	Document formal model for roles, characteristics
	16				X	Use formal specification language
	17				X	Document rationale consistently and completely
	18				X	Document formal model and functional spec
	19				X	Annotate source code with comments
	20				X	Document design and functional spec

Figure 34: Design Assurance

Secure module delivery, installation, and start-up will be demonstrated through documentation. Functional specification documents will illustrate the correspondence with the Security Policy. At level 3 and 4, high-level language implementations will be required for software and a high-level specification language will be used for any hardware components.

Guidance

An important aspect of design assurance is proper guidance to operators on how to operate the cryptographic module securely. Since these requirements are exclusively documentation requirements, the details will be given in the Documentation Requirements section of this chapter. Figure 35 provides a summary of the user and crypto officer guidance requirements.

	#	Security Level 1	2	3	4	Short Description
Guidance	21	X	X	X	X	Crypto officer guidance has functions, events
	22	X	X	X	X	Document secure admin procedures
	23	X	X	X	X	Document user behavior for secure operation
	24	X	X	X	X	Document user functions, ports and interfaces
	25	X	X	X	X	Document user responsibilities

Figure 35: Guidance

Mitigation of Other Attacks

The Security Policy will describe any specific attacks the cryptographic module is designed to mitigate and what measures the module uses. These other attacks are those that are not otherwise covered by the FIPS 140 security requirements but mitigated by the module under test. Some products include defenses against some sophisticated or device-specific attacks such as power or timing analysis. Figure 36 shows the one requirement for this section.

	#	Security Level 1	2	3	4	Short Description
Other	1	X	X	X	X	Security policy specify mitigation mechanisms

Figure 36: Mitigation of Other Attacks

Documentation Requirements

In order to pass the FIPS 140 validation, the cryptographic module implementation must not only provide the required security features and characteristics (e.g., public key cryptography and tamper-evident enclosures), but module documentation must also be presented to the testing laboratory to support many security claims. A Security Policy document is required to provide the framework and background for the module and the validation effort. Also, each of the 11 security requirement sections has documentation requirements.

Security Policy

The Security Policy document summarizes the cryptographic module's security claims and a version of it is made publicly available once the validation is complete. The purpose of a cryptographic module

Security Policy is to provide information to potential users to determine if the module will meet their organization's security policy. The Security Policy will describe the module's security features, capabilities, and access rights. The Derived Test Requirements for the Security Policy document is summarized in Figure 37 below.

	#	Security Level 1	2	3	4	Short Description
Security Policy	1	X	X	X	X	Security Policy included in documentation
	2	X	X	X	X	Security Policy contains rules
	3	X	X	X	X	Operator access, physical security, mitigations
	4	X	X	X	X	Crypto Module Security Policy
	5	X	X	X	X	Identification and authentication policy
	6	X	X	X	X	Access control policy
	7	X	X	X	X	Roles, services, keys
	8	X	X	X	X	Physical security policy
	9	X	X	X	X	Mitigation of other attacks policy

Figure 37: Security Policy

The Security Policy is expressed in terms of roles, services, cryptographic keys, and critical security parameters (CSP) and will contain the following policies:

- Identification and Authentication policy
- Access Control policy
- Physical Security policy
- Mitigation of Other Attacks policy

Identification and Authentication Policy

The Security Policy will specify an identification and authentication policy including:

- All operator roles (user, crypto officer, and maintenance)
- Types of authentication (identity-based or role-based)
- Required authentication data
- Strength of the authentication mechanism

Access Control Policy

The access control policy will identify the cryptographic keys and critical security parameters (CSP) that the operator has access to while performing a service and the type(s) of access the operator has to the parameters. The access control policy will include:

- All supported roles
- All of the services provided
- All of the cryptographic keys and CSPs used
- The services an operator can perform within an authorized role
- The type(s) of access to the keys and CSPs for each service within each role

Physical Security Policy

The physical security policy will include the physical security mechanisms that are implemented in a cryptographic module (e.g., tamper-evident seals, locks, tamper response and zeroization switches) and the actions required by the operator to ensure that physical security is maintained.

Mitigation of Other Attacks Policy

The Security Policy will document the mitigation of other attacks with the security mechanisms employed to mitigate those attacks if they are claimed as part of the validation.

Cryptographic Module Specification

The cryptographic module specification documentation will specify the hardware, software, and firmware components as well as the physical boundary and configuration of the module. If the cryptographic module includes software or firmware, the cryptographic boundary will include the hardware components that store and process the software and firmware.

The module documentation will identify the physical ports, logical interfaces, and all of the input and output data paths of the cryptographic module. It will also specify the controls, status indicators, and applicable physical, logical, and electrical characteristics.

A complete module block diagram will illustrate all of the major hardware components of the module and component interconnections. It will also include the design of the components of the cryptographic module. Figure 38 is an example of a block diagram of a cryptographic module.

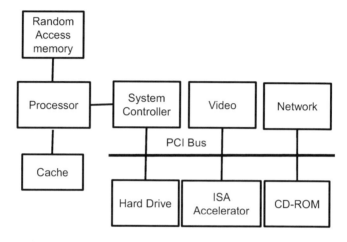

Figure 38: Example Block Diagram

The cryptographic module specification will describe all of the cryptographic functions and all of the associated security-related information including secret and private cryptographic keys and authentication data (e.g., passwords.)

Cryptographic Module Ports and Interfaces

The cryptographic module specification will include a description of all of the physical ports and logical interfaces. Documentation will also describe the input and output data paths.

There are four logical interfaces that must be described. These logical interfaces will be mapped to physical ports such as Ethernet ports or light emitting diode (LED) displays.

- Data input interface
- Data output interface
- Control input interface
- Status output interface

Roles, Services, and Authentication

All of the operator roles will be documented along with the services available for each role and the data required for operator authentication (if applicable).

Table 18 illustrates a sample mapping between operator roles and services available to authorized users in those roles.

Role	Associated Services
User	Configure module
	Initialize module
Crypto Officer	Generate AES keys
	Perform self-tests
	Zeroize keys

Table 18: Roles and Services

Finite State Model

The finite state model documentation will use state transition diagrams and/or state transition tables that describe all of the operational and error states, their corresponding state transitions, input events that trigger state transitions, and output events from those transitions. Figure 39 illustrates a simple example of a state transition diagram for 3 module states – inactive, active and self-test. Each state has input and output transitions depicted as labeled arrows. The arrows are labeled with the input or output data associated with the state transitions.

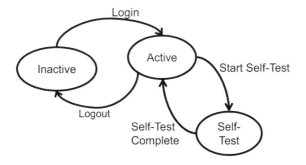

Figure 39: Example State Transition Diagram

121

Table 19 illustrates the previous state transition example in tabular form (state transition table). Each row in the table includes the current state, inputs to the state to trigger a state transition, output of the state transition, and the next state after the transition.

Current State	Input	Output	Next State
Inactive	Logout	Login	Active
Active	Login	Start Self-Test	Self-Test
Self-Test	Start Self-Test	Self-Test Complete	Inactive

Table 19: Sample State Transition Table

Physical Security

The physical implementation (or embodiment) of the cryptographic module will be documented. Cryptographic modules are classified in one of three categories:

1. Single-Chip
2. Multi-Chip Embedded
3. Multi-Chip Standalone

A single-chip embodiment is a single integrated circuit (IC) that may be physically secured by itself or with an enclosure. A multi-chip embedded module consists of two or more ICs that are embedded within an enclosure that may not be physically protected. A multi-chip standalone embodiment is a module made up of more than two ICs that are physically protected.

Documentation will include specifications for the physical security mechanisms used by the cryptographic module to protect all of the hardware, software, and firmware components as well as the cryptographic keys and critical security parameters. Depending on the embodiment type and security level, physical protection mechanisms may be tamper-evident seals and coatings or tamper-response mechanisms.

If a maintenance role is provided and physical access is required to fulfill that role, documentation will describe the physical maintenance access interface and maintenance access paths. The physical maintenance access interface may be a cover or door. Documentation will describe the physical security protection mechanisms used by the module such as tamper-evident seals on the doors or removable covers.

Operational Environment

The operational environment is the collection of functions necessary for the management of the module components. For most implementations, the underlying operating system is the critical part of the operating environment. For those products that do not have a general-purpose or otherwise modifiable operating system, many of the requirements in this section do not apply. The operational environment is classified in one of three categories:

1. General-Purpose
2. Modifiable
3. Limited

Both the general-purpose and modifiable operational environments allow for the re-configuration and the addition/deletion/modification of features, capabilities, and characteristics of the operational environment. Examples of general-purpose operational environments are general-purpose operating systems (e.g., Microsoft Windows or Linux). Modifiable operational environments may include operating systems in smart cards or programmable firmware. Special protections must be put in place to protect the cryptographic module from attacks from the operational environment.

Cryptographic modules using general–purpose or modifiable operational environments must meet the operating system security requirements within FIPS 140 and must be documented for the validation lab to review. FIPS 140-2 calls for Common Criteria (CC) evaluations at increasing CC evaluation assurance levels (EAL) depending upon the FIPS 140 security level. Table 20 summarizes the CC evaluation requirements by FIPS 140 security level.

Security Level	CC EAL	CC Protection Profiles
Level 1	N/A	N/A
Level 2	EAL 2	Controlled-Access or
Level 3	EAL 3+	Single-Level Operating System for
Level 4	EAL 4	Medium Robustness Environments

Table 20: Common Criteria Requirements

CC Protection Profile requirements are included in FIPS 140 Annex B [FIPS 140-2 B]. EAL 3+ refers to the standard Common Criteria

EAL 3 requirements plus the Trusted Path and Internal TOE Security Policy Model requirements.

Cryptographic Key Management

Cryptographic key management documentation describes the entire lifecycle of cryptographic keys, cryptographic key components, and critical security parameters used by the cryptographic module. Documentation will also describe the key management methods including: random number generation, key generation, key establishment, key distribution, key entry/output, key storage, and key zeroization.

Electro-Magnetic Interference/Compatibility (EMI/EMC)

Documented proof of the cryptographic module conforming to the applicable Title 47 Code of Federal Regulations, Part 15, Subpart B (Unintentional Radiators, Digital Devices) EMI/EMC requirements will be made available to the validation testing lab.

Class A requirements will be met for cryptographic modules pursuing security levels 1 and 2 validation and Class B requirements for levels 3 and 4.

Self-Tests

Documentation will describe all of the self-tests that will be performed by the module including power-up and conditional tests and the error states that the module can enter when a self-test fails. The conditions and actions necessary to exit the error states will be documented.

Design Assurance

Documentation for the design assurance processes describes the security characteristics of several aspects of the cryptographic module lifecycle including:

- Configuration Management
- Delivery and Operation
- Development
- Guidance Documentation

Configuration Management

Documentation will describe the configuration management (CM) system for the cryptographic module, module components, and the FIPS 140-related module documentation. The CM documentation shall include a configuration list of all hardware, software and firmware configuration items. The CM documentation will also describe the method used to uniquely identify each of the configuration items and their versions.

Delivery and Operation

The steps necessary for the secure delivery, installation, initialization, and start-up of the cryptographic module will be documented. These documents are similar to those required to satisfy the Lifecycle assurance class requirements in Common Criteria (CC) evaluations.

Development

To meet the development documentation requirements, documentation must describe how the hardware, software, and firmware designs correspond to the security policy/rules of operation of the cryptographic module. Testers will verify that each rule within the security policy is supported by the module's design.

Documentation will supply a list of all the hardware, software and firmware components contained in the cryptographic module. For software and firmware components, the documentation will include an annotated source listing of each of those components. For hardware components, a list of all of the hardware components contained in the cryptographic module will be provided. The tester will use this list to verify that the documentation includes schematics and/or Hardware Description Language (HDL) listings for the hardware components.

Functional specifications describe the cryptographic module, each external interface and port, and the purpose of each external interface.

At security level 4, a formal model documented in a formal specification language of the security policy of the cryptographic module is required. The formal model shall include a list of elements of the model, the operations performed on these elements, and the applicable security rules.

Guidance Documentation

There are two guidance documents required for FIPS 140 validation: crypto officer guidance and user guidance.

The crypto officer guidance specifies the administrative functions, security events, security parameters, physical ports, and logical interfaces of the cryptographic module available only to the crypto officer role. The guidance will include procedures on how to administer the cryptographic module securely.

The user guidance documents the approved security functions, physical ports, and logical interfaces available to the users of the cryptographic module. The user guidance will also describe the user responsibilities necessary for the secure operation of the module.

Mitigation of Other Attacks

Documentation will describe any attacks not covered by the FIPS 140 security requirements that the cryptographic module mitigates and what mechanisms are used to mitigate those attacks.

Summary

FIPS 140 security requirements are met by implementing standard security functions and characteristics in the cryptographic module in 11 areas for validation. Documentation accompanies the module to the validation testing lab to describe the module, its secure use, and to provide evidence for the security claims. The FIPS 140 Derived Test Requirements [DTR] document details the module features, vendor deliverables and lab testing requirements.

PART 3: REAL-WORLD EXAMPLES

In this part:

Chapter 9: Hardware Appliance

This chapter and the others in Part 3 of this book relate real-world examples of past FIPS 140 validation projects. The intent of these chapters is to explain in real terms what product developers can expect as they proceed through the FIPS 140 validation process. Each chapter focuses on a particular product type and highlights some of the unique characteristics of the FIPS 140 validation for those product types.

Hardware appliances (or multi-chip standalone hardware modules) account for over 40% of all FIPS 140 validations. These appliances include network routers, network switches, virtual private network (VPN) devices, firewalls, and a wide variety of other standalone devices that use cryptographic technologies to protect user data.

These hardware appliances often use application-specific integrated circuits (ASIC) and other purpose-built hardware components while leveraging some off-the-shelf components to produce a unique, competitive security platform. Application software and firmware in these appliances generally run on top of controlled or non-modifiable operating systems software (e.g., customized Linux). These appliances are designed to provide customers with high-performance and ease-of-use. The combination of specialized hardware and software deliver these valuable capabilities to users.

These products can give customers greater value by providing a level of assurance that the appliance's security functions perform properly. FIPS 140 validation provides that level of assurance in cryptographic functions and improves customer confidence that the appliance has been designed and implemented to meet industry standards. The FIPS 140 validation certificate indicates that the appliance has undergone independent scrutiny against vendor claims and has met the standards established by NIST.

FIPS 140 was initially developed with hardware devices in mind. The fact that there is a whole category of security requirements on physical security highlights this point. Figure 40 illustrates that according to the data provided by NIST [CMVL] as of December 2010, most hardware appliances have been validated to overall security level 2. Moreover, the cryptographic boundary for most hardware appliances is typically the entire product partly because the appliance physical enclosures can be designed to meet the level 2 physical security requirements.

While setting the cryptographic boundary around the entire hardware appliance may be an advantage in meeting the physical security requirements, it can be a disadvantage in other ways. By setting the cryptographic boundary around a specific appliance, the FIPS 140 certificate is only valid for that specific model and version. As the appliance is modified, updated, and upgraded, the FIPS 140 validation will need to be maintained if not re-validated entirely. Careful consideration should be taken for assessing the initial validation effort against future re-validation and maintenance.

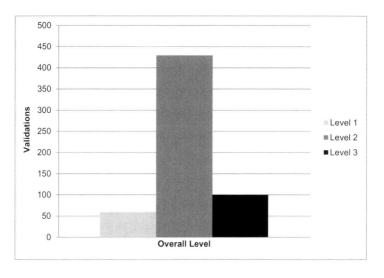

Figure 40: Hardware Appliances

Physical Security

Perhaps one of the most nettlesome FIPS 140 physical security requirements for hardware appliances is the opacity requirement. Hardware appliance developers spend a disproportionate amount of time and money on this one FIPS 140 requirement. The concept behind the opacity requirement as it relates to hardware appliances is to prevent attackers from gaining insights into the cryptographic module internals by being able to identify its hardware components. The assumption is that if an attacker can identify what integrated circuits and other hardware components are used in the module, they could learn something that could be used to compromise the module. For this reason, Section 5.1 of the Implementation Guidance [IG] entitled "Opacity and Probing of Cryptographic Modules with Fans, Ventilation Holes or Slits at Level 2" was developed to more fully describe the requirements and testing procedures used to assess the cryptographic module for physical security.

Hardware appliances typically have ventilation slits or holes and fans to provide ventilation for heat dissipation of the electronic components. FIPS 140 physical requirements state that the module must be opaque within the visible spectrum. For appliances, opacity means that if someone can read part or chip numbers with a flashlight and the naked eye looking through the ventilation holes (as depicted in Figure 41), then the module will fail the opacity test. Clearly ¼ inch vent holes are too big, allowing someone to see the part numbers. Much smaller vent holes could prevent someone from seeing the part numbers; however, smaller vent holes may have a thermal impact and could cause the appliance to overheat.

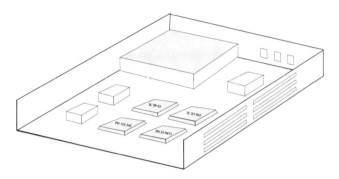

Figure 41: Ventilation Holes

Opacity can be a major issue for appliance developers during the FIPS 140 validation process. The difficulty for developers arises when the hardware appliances are not designed with FIPS 140 requirements in mind, so considering opacity/physical security requirements in product design is important. Some vendors have developed "FIPS 140 kits" as field serviceable items which can be added to standard appliance enclosures to provide the necessary tamper-evidence and opacity. These kits amount to add-ons that can be applied by the customer interested in meeting the FIPS 140 requirements.

The other issue related to opacity is that the testing for opacity is handled inconsistently across different testing labs. A design that may be considered adequate to meet the opacity requirements by one lab may not be considered adequate by another testing lab.

In addition to opacity requirements, appliances pursuing security level 2 are required to provide evidence of tampering if the module is compromised by the removal of covers, line cards, modular port interfaces, etc. Tamper-evident seals must be placed over these access points, and most appliances do not normally ship with suitable solutions. As such, a "FIPS kit" can provide specialized seals that an end user can install by following guidance provided in the Security Policy.

Self-Tests

Self-tests are another issue for all validations, but especially for hardware because self-tests must be built into the hardware and cannot be easily "bolted on" after the module has been implemented. Chapter 8: Security Requirements reviewed all of the FIPS 140 security requirements, which included the self-test category with power-up and conditional self-tests.

Power-up self-tests are run when the module is powered up or when requested by an authorized operator. These tests are known-answer tests for all of the supported cryptographic functions. They will also include integrity checks for any software and/or firmware used in the cryptographic module to ensure that the code has not been compromised.

So-called conditional self-tests are tests on optional cryptographic functions such as key management and bypass capabilities. If public or private keys are used, then the conditional self-tests must perform a pair-wise encryption/decryption test. If the module offers a bypass capability, then there must be a self-test to check the switching from normal cryptographic operation to bypass mode.

Bypass self-tests can be a big issue. Virtual private network (VPN) router products oftentimes include bypass capabilities, so self-tests must be provided. However, bypass self-tests are normally not implemented for performance reasons unless FIPS 140 requirements are firmly included in the engineering design requirements.

Ports and Interfaces

One of the easier security requirement categories for hardware appliances to address is defining ports and interfaces. If the cryptographic boundary is the entire appliance product, the ports are the physical ports used to input and output cryptographic information. RJ-11 Ethernet or universal serial bus (USB) ports and a power port are typical ports on an appliance. Light-emitting diode (LED) displays are common output ports for status information.

The cryptographic Security Policy will map the physical ports to the logical data input, data output, control input and status output interfaces. Some of the ports such as the Ethernet port may serve multiple interfaces. That is, the Ethernet port can be used for inputting data as well as outputting data.

Roles, Services and Authentication

FIPS 140 requires that there are at least two authorized user roles for each cryptographic module. The Crypto Officer Role will generally fulfill the cryptographic administration functions. The User Role executes the general cryptographic functions such as encrypting and decrypting data. These users will login, usually with user name and password to the appliance to authenticate them in order to perform their tasks. A unique user name (e.g., "jdoe") will facilitate meeting security level 3 for this section. Users may also be other IT systems or programs.

Operational Environment

Most hardware appliances use some form of customized operating system such as a version of Linux. These embedded operating systems are not considered by FIPS 140 testing labs or NIST to be general-purpose and are thus not subject to any of the security requirements in the Operational Environment category of FIPS 140. Most hardware appliances are able to claim that this category is "not applicable."

EMI/EMC

Electro-magnetic interference and electro-magnetic compatibility (EMI/EMC) requirements are met by running standard Federal Communication Commission (FCC) tests. Title 47 Code of Federal Regulations, Part 15, Subpart B, Unintentional Radiators, Digital Devices, Class A (i.e., for business use) define the tests that will satisfy FIPS 140 level 1 and 2 requirements.

Protecting CSPs

Cryptographic modules must protect critical security parameters (CSP) even during and after system failure. Some systems may dump diagnostic information after a system failure. This diagnostic information is important to the product vendor as well as the customer to help them recover from the failure and prevent future problems. However, the FIPS 140 key management security requirements include the need for the module to prevent the inadvertent disclosure of cryptographic keys and other security parameters.

A common diagnostic procedure used by appliances is to dump system information upon system failure. This dump may include memory contents and configuration information. Since system failures are unexpected, diagnostic dumps tend to contain comprehensive system information in order to give diagnosticians as much information as possible. If the system dump is completely indiscriminate, the dump may contain security-relevant information. Appliance designers should consider providing a provision to limit the type of information that will be provided in diagnostic dumps in order not to include security information.

Validate an Appliance Family

A good tip for hardware appliance developers interested in maintaining the "shelf life" of the module validation and improve the return on their validation investment should consider validating a "family" of appliances that share cryptographic features. Defining an appropriate cryptographic boundary is the key to achieving this goal.

The notion of defining a cryptographic boundary such that the module can be used across many products over an extended period of time is easy to envision when the module is a PCI card or software library. These modules can be embedded or integrated into other products or systems and can remain unchanged and intact for an extended period of time. The products using the FIPS 140 validated cryptographic module will certainly meet the spirit of FISMA, NSTISSP #11 and other regulations requiring the use of FIPS 140 validated cryptographic modules. What is less clear is when the cryptographic module is a standalone hardware appliance enclosed in a physical case. This standalone module will not be embedded or integrated into another system and thus its FIPS 140 validation will not be shared with other products.

What has become more common practice among hardware appliance developers is to submit a family of appliances to FIPS 140 validation at the same time. These appliances share a common cryptographic core and set of platforms. By submitting a family or set of appliances at the same time, the developer reduces redundant effort and time. The key to being able to accomplish this is to leverage the cryptographic module components across a number of individual appliances. Using the same integrated circuits and software that perform the FIPS 140 approved cryptographic functions will ensure that the family of appliances can be validated together.

Oftentimes, hardware appliance models within a family differ in their bandwidth, throughput, number of ports, memory size, and additional features; but the underlying cryptographic features and implementation are identical across all of the models. As long as the cryptographic module boundary is defined identically across all models in the family of appliances submitted for FIPS 140 validation, all of the appliances can be recognized in the validation. While this situation is a bit different from sharing a cryptographic chip, board or software library across a number of products over time, validating a family of appliances at the same time does save time and effort.

Summary

Hardware appliance developers face unique issues during the preparation for FIPS 140 validations. Physical security requirements, in particular opacity requirements, present some challenges for developers who have not designed their appliance products with FIPS 140 requirements in mind. Meeting product enclosure ventilation and thermal control demands may conflict with the FIPS 140 opacity requirements. Ventilation holes may not be so big as to enable an attacker to identify the internal components of the cryptographic module.

FIPS 140 self-test requirements must be considered in the design of any cryptographic modules to meet the FIPS 140 requirements, but hardware appliances especially must be designed with these self-tests at the outset.

Validating a family of appliances at one time is a good way to reduce the redundant effort of submitting individual appliances to the FIPS 140 validation process. The key to successfully saving time and effort is to define the cryptographic boundary carefully to ensure that all of the necessary components and features are included in each appliance in the family.

Chapter 10: Security Software Application

Consumers, commercial enterprises and government are growing more and more dependent upon software to provide services and functions to carry on their day-to-day activities. Software company sales revenues reflect this trend. Microsoft Corporation reported revenues of over $62B for the fiscal year ending June 2010 and Oracle Corporation reported over $27B in revenues. A growing subset of the software business is the software security business made up of companies such as McAfee, Symantec and RSA Security (the security division of EMC). Security software such as anti-virus, firewalls, virtual private networks (VPN), and anti-spyware products protect desktops, networks, and servers for all types of users. This market segment is expected to exceed $16B in 2010.

With the growth in the use of software, it is natural that the number of software modules submitted to FIPS 140 has also grown. Figure 42 shows the number of software module FIPS 140 validations over the years. Overall, nearly 30% of all FIPS 140 validations are software module validations.

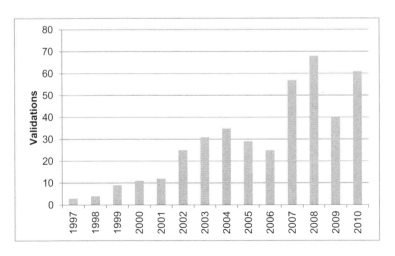

Figure 42: Software Validations By Year

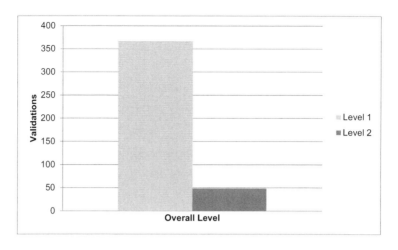

Figure 43: Software Modules

Overall Level 2

Figure 43 illustrates that software cryptographic modules are generally validated at overall security level 1. For most software modules, meeting the FIPS 140 requirements for overall security level 1 is relatively straightforward. Meeting overall security level 2 however is more challenging for software modules. However, there have been a number of validations completed at level 2. One reason some product vendors chose to pursue overall level 2 is customer demand.

In 2007, the U.S. Army Letter to Industry [Army] stated that all information assurance (IA) and IA-enabled products using encryption must use hardware, software or firmware modules that have FIPS 140-2 overall level 2 validation. The Army letter detailed the requirements for products to be listed on the Army's IA Approved Products List (APL). Army organizations were instructed to purchase only those products on the APL, so it was important for product vendors to have their products included on the APL.

Gaining an overall level 2 FIPS 140 validation for software modules is difficult, but the Army represented some very significant sales opportunities. Competing product vendors developed and submitted software modules to FIPS 140 validation level 2 with an eye towards winning more business from the Army.

Operational Environment

For all standalone and embedded hardware modules, FIPS 140 Operational Environment security requirements are generally not applicable. These cryptographic modules can ignore this category of requirements because they do not run on general-purpose or modifiable operating systems. Software modules, however generally do run on general-purpose operating systems. Operational Environment security level 2 requires that the cryptographic module be under the control of an operating system evaluated at Common Criteria (CC) Evaluation Assurance Level (EAL) 2. Moreover, the FIPS 140 validation platforms must coincide with the CC evaluated platforms. This means that the hardware compute platform used in the CC evaluation (e.g., HP Proliant DL365 G5 Server platform running an AMD Opteron processor) must be the same platform used in the FIPS 140 validation.

The validation platform must also be tested against the Federal Communications Commission (FCC) Title 47 Code of Federal Regulations, Part15, Subpart B, Class A requirements in order to meet the FIPS 140 Electromagnetic Interference/Electromagnetic Compatibility (EMI/EMC) requirements.

Both the Operational Environment and EMI/EMC requirements seem contradictory for a cryptographic module whose boundary is defined by the software only. Nonetheless, the convention is for software modules to claim Physical Security requirements as "not applicable", but still claim conformance to the Operational Environment and EMI/EMC requirements.

Cryptographic Boundary

Establishing a well-defined cryptographic module boundary is mandatory for any FIPS 140 validation effort. Commercial product vendors should also be interested in constraining the cryptographic boundary in order to minimize the monetary and effort investments. Software products, especially security products, may contain a wide variety of cryptographic features, but only a few may directly impact the customer. To minimize the FIPS 140 validation costs, focus the validation effort on customer-related functions only.

Security products such as anti-virus (AV) packages may use cryptographic functions to encrypt communications between the administrator's console and the server. The AV product may also use cryptographic techniques to protect the product from piracy. While these are useful management functions within the AV product, they have little direct impact on the end user/customer. The end user probably only wants to make sure that the AV signature updates are delivered securely. In that regard, the digital signatures within the AV signature updates are the main cryptographic function the end user cares about. This cryptographic feature should be the focus of the FIPS 140 validation.

Security product vendors tend to focus on security and might include too many cryptographic functions in the module boundary thus increasing the scope of the effort and increasing the time and costs. Security product vendors also tend to focus too much attention on vulnerabilities they may uncover in the process of preparing for the FIPS 140 validation. For example, potential weaknesses in the authentication mechanisms may be a concern for penetration testers but not FIPS 140 testers. There is a difference between security and FIPS 140 validation. In pursuing FIPS 140 validation, product vendors need to focus on validation, not security. This means focusing effort on the issues directly related to meeting the FIPS 140 security requirements and setting aside (for the moment) any other security issues that might be uncovered.

Hardware appliances tend to claim the entire product as the cryptographic boundary in order to help meet the overall level 2 requirements; by doing that, hardware modules also restrict the "shelf life" of their FIPS 140 validation. Hardware changes over time would force some form of re-validation. With the shortened product lifecycles, FIPS 140 validations for hardware appliances may only last a year or so. Software modules with a carefully defined cryptographic boundary can extend the length of time of the FIPS 140 validation by constraining the boundary to a core, unchanging set of code. The validated software module can then be used in multiple versions or generations of other products.

Even if software (or hardware) updates are required, a validation maintenance plan can help ease the re-validation burden and increase the validation "shelf life." Refer to Chapter 14: Best Practices for more on developing an effective validation maintenance program.

Design Assurance

The Software Security category of FIPS 140-1 was updated and renamed to the Design Assurance security category in FIPS 140-2, so the requirements in this category are focused on software development security. For security level 2 in the Design Assurance category, the following requirements apply:

- Implement configuration management
- Use unique identifiers for each configuration item
- Document secure installation setup
- Document secure distribution and delivery
- Document design and security policy
- Document source code for components
- Documentation includes functional specification

These requirements are a subset of CC EAL 2 requirements and are generally met by commercial software developers as a normal part of the product development process. If the cryptographic module has undergone CC evaluation, the configuration management (CM), delivery, installation, and functional specification (FSP) documents may be reused to meet the FIPS 140 requirements.

One requirement that causes some concern is the source code requirement. In spite of any confidential disclosure agreements established between the product developer and the testing lab, some product developers become overly cautious about allowing access to product source code fearing that some of their intellectual property might be leaked. By the very nature of validation and the need for the testers to "look under the hood", source code review of some kind is required. Product developers can satisfy their corporate security objectives by holding the source code review at the product developer's site. Testers can come to the product development site and under direct supervision, conduct the source code review. The source code will not leave the premises and the testers will be under scrutiny at all times.

Summary

The purchase and use of software-based security applications has been growing in government and private sectors and so have FIPS 140 validations of software modules. Most FIPS 140 validations of software modules are at overall level 1, but some have been validated at level 2. Meeting the overall level 2 requirements present some special challenges including operating system and platform restrictions, cryptographic boundary considerations, and design assurance requirements.

Overall level 2 requirements can be met with careful planning and a solid understanding of the FIPS 140 requirements.

Chapter 11: Data Encryption Library

The National Security Telecommunications and Information Systems Security Policy (NSTISSP) #11 and other government regulations require government entities to only purchase products that contain cryptographic modules with FIPS 140 validations. This means that those products may be validated themselves or they may integrate modules that have been FIPS 140 validated. Either way, the customer's objective is met - to gain a level of confidence that the encryption technologies used by the products they purchase are implemented securely using approved algorithms.

The previous chapter outlined some unique characteristics of FIPS 140 validations for security software applications. These software products were submitted as complete standalone modules to the FIPS 140 validation process. Some cryptographic software modules (libraries) are intended to be integrated with other software to produce an application product. Original equipment manufacturer (OEM) providers develop software components such as encryption libraries that are designed for integration with application software. Application software developers may also develop encryption libraries for their reuse across multiple products in a product line. These software libraries can be FIPS 140 validated and the products integrating these libraries will satisfy the government regulations for using FIPS 140 validated modules.

Encryption libraries are linked in with software applications to provide cryptographic functions. Although the library is intended to be linked with other application software, cryptographic libraries are generally submitted to the FIPS 140 validation as multi-chip, standalone modules as are all other software modules.

Ports and Interfaces

Commercial OEM encryption libraries are intended to be integrated and used by application software developers. In order for application developers to use the libraries, the application programmatic interfaces (API) must be well documented. The API documentation must describe the function calls, input and output variables, and other use parameters. This API documentation along with a mapping to the appropriate FIPS 140 interface (e.g., data input, data output, control input, and status output) generally will satisfy the FIPS 140 requirements for the Ports and Interfaces category. Physical ports in this instance will refer to the ports on the host computer including the computer's keyboard, network, and USB ports.

Physical Security

Since software libraries have no physical embodiment, the FIPS 140 Physical Security requirements do not apply to the software itself but to the host computer upon which the module is tested. To meet the security level 1 requirements, the computer platform must have a hard plastic or metal, commercial-grade enclosure. Virtually any commercial computer enclosure will meet these FIPS 140 requirements.

OEM vendors seek to sell as many copies of their libraries as possible. Likewise, application software developers that develop encryption libraries want to be able to maximize the use of the FIPS 140 validated libraries across several products. To accomplish this, software libraries will generally be validated at Physical Security level 1 because level 1 enables the broadest platform applicability. Many of the OEM libraries have been tested on a wide variety of hardware (and operating system) platforms to maximize the coverage.

Operational Environment

Software encryption libraries, like application software will be run on general-purpose operating systems. This makes them subject to the requirements in the FIPS 140 Operational Environment category. As with the Physical Security category requirements, software libraries will generally pursue level 1 validation in the Operational Environment category to maximize the applicability to a variety of platforms. Many FIPS 140 validated software libraries have been tested with a variety of operating systems. This enables application developers to use the FIPS 140 validated libraries and claim conformance to the government regulations requiring the use of FIPS 140 validated cryptographic modules.

From the application developer's perspective, an issue that frequently arises is when the OEM vendor's library did not test the library on the operating system platform that the application developer needs to support. For example, a software virtual private network (VPN) product runs on the Windows 7 operating system, but the encryption library that is used in the application has only been FIPS 140 validated on legacy

Windows XP. The VPN product cannot claim conformance to the government regulations requiring the use of FIPS 140 validated crypto-graphic modules. The VPN developer either has to coax the library provider to re-test the library using the Windows 7 operating system or submit their VPN product to FIPS 140 validation. Chapter 15: Issues With FIPS 140 will discuss this issue in more depth, but in order for the VPN product to claim compliance with the government regulations, the encryption library must have been tested on the same operating system as the VPN product.

Validation Maintenance Program

In order to address the Operational Environment platform sup-port issue mentioned earlier, encryption library OEM providers need to have a validation maintenance plan to keep FIPS 140 validations up-to-date with the latest code versions. This plan should take into account the popularity of the various operating systems and operating system versions. The validation maintenance plan should also consider the timing and coordination with operating system revisions as well as encryption library revisions.

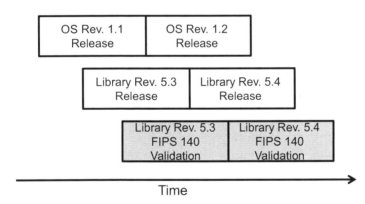

Figure 44: Validation Maintenance

Figure 44 depicts an example validation maintenance schedule coordinated with key supported operating system releases. Prior to OS Revision 1.1 release, the OEM encryption library provider should ideally be able to develop Library Revision 5.3 to support the new OS release. When the Library Revision 5.3 is ready, it can be submitted to the FIPS

140 testing with OS Revision 1.1. Once the FIPS 140 validation has completed, application developers can use Library Revision 5.3 on OS Revision 1.1 and claim conformance with the government regulations.

For OEM vendors and the benefit of their application developer customers, it is important that Library Revision 5.4 is updated for OS Revision 1.2 and submitted for FIPS 140 re-validation. This validation maintenance plan will enable existing application development customers to keep up with the latest supported operating system and library releases and attract new application development customers that are developing products on the latest platforms.

Summary

Encryption libraries face similar challenges as application software products with the FIPS 140 validation process. While physical security requirements relate directly to the hardware upon which the software encryption library executes, the FIPS 140 validation is only valid on the computer hardware that was used in the testing. Similarly, the library's FIPS 140 validation is only applicable to the operating systems and versions that were used during the testing. In addition, successful OEM encryption libraries vendors will have in place a sound validation maintenance program to ensure that their customer needs are well-served.

Chapter 12: USB Flash Drive

In November 2008, the U.S. Department of Defense (DOD) was inflected by a worm named Conficker, a variant of the W32.SillyFDC worm. This worm affected the DOD Non-Classified Internet Protocol Router Network (NIPRNet) and the Secret Internet Protocol Router Network (SIPRNet) and was allegedly propagated by removable storage media such as USB flash drives. This prompted the DOD to ban the use of USB storage devices until a realistic mitigation strategy could be developed. The ban lasted 15 months until the DOD decided that the USB storage devices were so pervasive that they had to continue their use. USB drives made it easy for DOD personnel to transfer large amounts of data to remote sites where network bandwidth was severely limited (e.g., ships at sea).

The Defense Information Systems Agency (DISA) developed the Joint Task Force – Global Networks Operation (JTF-GNO) Communications Tasking Order (CTO) 09-xxx as guidance for the implementation and use of portable electronic devices including USB flash storage drives. One of the key requirements was that the USB drives be encrypted with FIPS 140 compliant encryption. The best and easiest way to demonstrate compliance to this order is to use USB storage devices that have FIPS 140 validations.

USB storage drive vendors interested in selling their products to the DOD and potentially "locking out" the competition aggressively pursued FIPS 140 validation for their devices. Some vendors pursued the higher (level 2 and 3) overall security levels meaning the products needed to have tamper detection/protection mechanisms. The DOD episode illustrates the business opportunities that can arise when the government develops procurement policies that affect product design, implementation, and testing.

Validation Maintenance Planning

USB flash memory devices are mobile, versatile, and inexpensive. The growth of the USB flash memory drive business can be at least partly attributed to the ease-of-use and ubiquity of the USB interface. The increase in flash memory chip capacity has also fueled the demand for these devices. Only a few years ago, 1 GB flash memory devices were expensive and difficult to find. Now, 8GB drives cost under $20 and there are USB flash drives with 256GB capacity. In this rapidly growing market, new products are constantly emerging; this means that in order to remain competitive, device vendors must rapidly update their products and provide new and enhanced capabilities. Many of the changes affect the controller chip in the USB storage device.

Figure 45 shows a simplified diagram of a typical USB flash memory device pointing out the USB interface, controller and flash memory chips. The controller chip, located between the USB interface and memory chip, manages the data and control functions to the memory. For most FIPS 140 validations of USB flash memory devices, the cryptographic boundary has been defined as the entire device. This means that any changes to the controller chip would invalidate the FIPS 140 validation for the module. Since many USB device revisions involve changes to the controller, re-validation is necessary to maintain the FIPS 140 validation.

USB memory devices now change so frequently that by the time a validation is completed the product is obsolete because the controller changes for the next revision of the product. These devices need a solid re-validation plan.

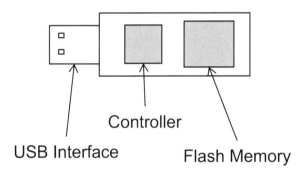

Controller

USB Interface   Flash Memory

Figure 45: USB Flash Drive

Physical Security

USB flash memory devices meet the FIPS 140 physical security requirements with the device's case or enclosure since the cryptographic boundary is generally the entire device. Many of the FIPS 140 valida-tions of these devices are for overall level 2. Level 2 requirements for physical security can be met by using an opaque enclosure over the device and some sort of tamper evidence seal. Since most commercially-available USB flash drives use an opaque case, meeting this requirement is easy, and there are several ways to fulfill the requirement for tamper evidence.

Some vendors chose to pursue an overall level 3. Physical security at level 3 requires the use of a hard potting material such that any attempt to breach the potting material would damage the module. Usually some kind of epoxy is used to encase the USB device.

While there are no formal government regulations for the FIPS 140 level 3 validation, some vendors have chosen to gain level 3 validation for competitive reasons. FIPS 140 level 3 validation indicates that the product meets more stringent requirements than level 2 including physical security and clearly differentiates the product from many of the others. This fact can be used for marketing and advertising purposes.

Self-Tests

Self-tests are an issue for all hardware devices if these tests are not designed and built into the module. USB flash memory devices are no exception. Depending upon the functionality provided by the device, a set of power-up and conditional self-tests must be executed.

Power-up self-tests are executed on module initialization and on demand by the Crypto Officer. Should any of the self-tests fail, the module will not initialize nor will any of the cryptographic services be available to any of the users. The self-tests must include known answer tests (KAT) for each FIPS 140 approved algorithms supported by the module. A KAT executes the cryptographic algorithm on data for which the correct output is already known and compares the calculated output with the previously generated output (the known answer). If the calculated output does not equal the known answer, the KAT fails.

Another power-up self-test is the software/firmware integrity test using an error detection code (EDC) that is executed against all validated software and firmware components in the cryptographic module. If the calculated EDC does not match the expected value, the integrity test fails.

Conditional tests include: pair-wise consistency tests, software/firmware load tests, manual key entry tests, continuous random number generator tests, and bypass tests. Depending on the specific functions provided by the cryptographic module, some of these tests do not apply. For example, most USB devices have no bypass mechanism, so the bypass conditional self-tests are not applicable.

Algorithm Testing

A key tip for USB flash memory device developers: be sure algorithm testing does not hold up the process. Cryptographic algorithm tests for each FIPS 140 approved algorithm supported by the module are a prerequisite for any FIPS 140 module validation. These algorithm tests must be run and validated each time the device controller changes because the so-called "environment" changes. When the environment changes the algorithms have to be re-tested.

Part of the validation maintenance program planning should include timing and scheduling for algorithm re-validation when the device controller changes.

Summary

USB flash memory devices have demonstrated their popularity and utility in not only the private sector, but in the government as well. As evidenced by the DOD incident in 2008, it is apparent that these electronic storage devices serve an important function. FIPS 140 cryptographic validation of these devices enhances their value by assuring customers that the encryption technologies used within them have been tested against industry standards.

For USB flash memory device vendors, the key to remaining competitive with FIPS 140 validations is to have a sound validation maintenance plan that takes into account the rapid product lifecycles and the length of typical FIPS 140 validations. Some vendors have chosen to invest in and pursue FIPS 140 overall level 3 validations to gain competitive advantage and differentiation in the marketplace.

Chapter 13: Open Source Library

Open source software is attractive to end users because of the potential cost savings over commercially licensed software. It also has appeal because it is produced by a community of developers with lots of new ideas and an unparalleled devotion to the craft of improving software. The U.S. Government recognizes the attractiveness of open source software and wants to take advantage of the benefits this source of technology can offer. Reducing cost and increasing competitiveness and effectiveness make open source an attractive alternative to traditional commercial software products.

Open source software is attractive to application developers because it reduces development time and costs. Application developers can integrate the open source software for minimal or no licensing costs and be able to offer capabilities almost immediately in their products. By using open source software, application developers minimize the time to "climb the learning curve" to develop technical expertise in the functional area. This can be a significant savings for cryptographic technologies which requires some detailed, in-depth knowledge that can be difficult to acquire.

OpenSSL Project

The OpenSSL Project [OpenSSL] is a collaborative effort to develop a robust, commercial-grade, full featured open source toolkit implementing the Secure Sockets Layer (SSL) and Transport Layer Security (TLS) protocols as well as a general purpose cryptography library. The project is managed by a worldwide community of volunteers to plan and develop the OpenSSL toolkit. The OpenSSL toolkit is licensed under an arrangement such that developers are free to use it for commercial and non-commercial purposes. The toolkit includes a set of application programmatic interfaces (API) along with comprehensive developer documentation for software developers to build complete applications that use cryptographic functionality. For example, OpenSSL is used in a variety of commercial security products to encrypt data in transit and at rest. Developers compile the OpenSSL source and link the library into their applications to utilize the cryptographic functions.

Openssl FIPS Object Module

The Open Source Software Institute [OSSI] has taken the lead in shepherding subsets of OpenSSL distributions through the FIPS 140 validation process. The validation efforts are sponsored by multiple government and industry entities and managed through OSSI. OSSI is the "vendor of record" and the coordinating body for the validated modules. The module that has been FIPS 140 validated is called the OpenSSL FIPS Object Module (OFOM). The first FIPS 140 validation for OFOM occurred in 2006.

The initial OFOM FIPS 140 validation took over 5 years to complete because this project was breaking new ground for the testing labs and NIST since OFOM was the first FIPS 140 validation based on source code. In order to fit into the FIPS 140 testing paradigm, there was a great deal of discussing and testing to resolve the issues they encountered.

According to the OFOM Security Policy [OFOM SP] the OFOM has been validated to FIPS 140-2 overall level 1 and supports the following cryptographic algorithms:

- Triple DES
- Rivest Shamir Adleman (RSA)
- Diffie-Hellman
- Advanced Encryption Standard (AES)
- Secure Hashing Algorithm (SHA)
- Keyed-Hash Message Authentication Code (HMAC)
- Random Number Generator (RNG)

In addition to the OFOM Security Policy, OSSI published the OFOM User Guide [OFOM UG] as a technical reference for developers using the OFOM and to provide more detailed explanation of the Security Policy. The OFOM User Guide provides detailed instructions to software developers on how to generate the object module identifying supported hardware platforms, operating systems, and build commands. The OFOM User Guide even has specific instructions on the proper delivery of the source code. The API documentation provides the function calls for the cryptographic functions, setting the module to FIPS mode, and executing power-up self-tests. This user guide includes topics such as:

- FIPS OpenSSL Integrity Tests and Integrity Chain
- Compatible Platforms
- Generating the FIPS OpenSSL Object Module
- Creating Applications Using the FIPS OpenSSL Object Module
- OpenSSL FIPS Application Programmatic Interface

The FIPS 140 standard requires an integrity test of cryptographic modules to verify their integrity at initialization. Most FIPS 140 validated software modules consist of a pre-built binary executable, so they implement the module integrity check as a digest check over portions of the executable file. Because the OFOM is built from source code, the FIPS 140 integrity check is a chain of digest checks beginning with the source files used for the FIPS 140 validation testing. There are build time, link time, and run time integrity checks in the chain. The OFOM User Guide provides useful and detailed information for software developers that enable them to compile, build, link, and run the OFOM in the FIPS 140 approved manner.

According to the NIST CMVP FAQ [CMVP FAQ], a FIPS 140 validated cryptographic (hardware, software, firmware, or hybrid) module may be integrated or embedded into another product. While a product which uses an embedded FIPS 140 validated cryptographic module cannot claim itself to be validated; it can claim that it utilizes an embedded FIPS 140 validated cryptographic module or "FIPS 140 compliance." This applies to OFOM as well. Modules generated in accordance with the guidance in the OFOM Security Policy and OFOM User Guide can be "vendor affirmed" to be FIPS 140-2 compliant when running on supported computer systems. While "vendor affirmed" may not be the same as "FIPS validated", from a security perspective it serves the same purpose – using a FIPS 140 validated module to perform cryptographic functions.

The other option available to developers using OFOM is to pursue "private label" validations under the developer's name. Private label validations integrate OFOM source code into the developer's product or library and are FIPS 140 tested as binary objects on developer-specified target platforms. There have been several FIPS 140 validations of other modules and products that incorporated the OFOM source code. The FIPS 140 certificates are listed under the names of the other products and vendors on the NIST FIPS 140 module validation list website [CMVL].

Re-Validations

OFOM has completed several validations and re-validations since 2006 thanks in large part to government, corporate sponsorships, and the leadership of OSSI. Table 21 summarizes the FIPS 140 certificates the OFOM has received

Certificate Number	Version	Validation Dates
642	1.0	2/06, 3/06, 6/06
733	1.1.1	2/07, 11/07
918	1.1.2	2/08
1051	1.2	11/08, 11/09
1111	1.2	4/09, 5/10

Table 21: OFOM FIPS 140 certificates

OSSI continues to seek additional sponsorship to renew the OFOM FIPS 140 validations in order to keep the most current version possible available for developers. These validations would be shared with the community and would increase the applicability of the OFOM. Since FIPS 140 validations testing can cost $30,000 or more, some form of sponsorship is needed.

Delays In NIST Validations

Product developers are constantly driving to meet (or shorten) timelines to address customer needs and competitive pressures. Lengthy or delayed FIPS 140 validation projects could have a negative impact on product sales revenues. Chapter 7: Costs and Timelines reviewed the FIPS 140 validation phases and the estimated time each phase can take. Product developers, FIPS 140 consultants, and testing labs can manage the time it takes to complete their phases, but have no control over the time NIST takes to complete the final validation phase. The NIST validation phase is sub-divided into four sub-phases. The sub-phases and their estimated durations are summarized in Table 22.

154

Validaton Sub-Phase	Estimated Duration
Review Pending	2 - 3 months
Review	2 weeks
Coordination	1 – 2 weeks
Finalization	2 weeks

Table 22: NIST Phases

The estimates show that it can take over 4 months for NIST to complete their validation of the testing lab results with half of the time waiting for NIST resources to become available to begin the review process. While Table 22 illustrates time estimates, the variances can be great and unpredictable. The OpenSSL FIPS Object Module re-validations have experienced several occasions where the NIST validation phase took an unexpected amount of time.

The interval between the time the testing lab submitted their test results to NIST and the time to final validation was seven months for Certificate #1051. The interval for Certificate #1111 was 13 months. More recent validations have taken less time, but product developers should be aware of such uncontrollable variances in the FIPS 140 validation process and try to plan accordingly.

Summary

OSSI and the OpenSSL FIPS Object Module have blazed a trail for open source cryptographic modules. It has taken a great deal of time and effort on the parts of OSSI members, sponsors, NIST, and other government experts to enable application vendors to "affirm" that their applications meet the FIPS 140 requirements by using the OpenSSL FIPS Object Module. Product developers also have the option to pursue "private label" FIPS 140 validations using the Open SSL FIPS Object Module source code to build the cryptographic module and test it under their own name.

PART 4: CONCLUSIONS

In this part:

Chapter 14: Best Practices

The objective of product developers is to successfully meet the FIPS 140 security and validation requirements while minimizing time and cost investments. Best practices are those activities that have proven most effective towards meeting these validation objectives. Best practices have been proven with a broad range of product types, business situations, and operational environments. Through the experiences of many FIPS 140 projects the following best practices have emerged:

- Consider FIPS 140 requirements at the product design phase
- Track and manage customer expectations
- Identify an internal advocate for the validation project
- Educate all levels of the organization on FIPS 140
- Develop a validation maintenance program
- Follow sound project management practices
- Work with trusted partners

Consider FIPS 140 Requirements at Product Design

Several FIPS 140 security requirements require that the cryptographic module have some very specific functionality such as tamper-evident seals or tamper-response mechanisms. Some of these features can be "bolted on" after the module has been designed and built. Other security requirements such as hardware self-tests must be designed into the product.

Building the cryptographic module with FIPS 140 security requirements in mind is a key best practice in security certification planning and has many components, ranging from product design to budgeting and resource planning. When executed properly, this concept can greatly reduce the time, cost, and burden of FIPS 140 validation. Resources can be scheduled to develop the required functionality and to support the effort (via availability for questions, code reviews, etc.) to move forward. When budgets are planned and approved, the acquisition and approval process is optimized (which means contracts are signed faster), purchase orders are delivered faster the product is submitted for testing faster which leads to increased revenue.

Product developers want to avoid situations where the FIPS 140 validation project is stalled because the module under test lacks a key feature necessary to meet a FIPS 140 security requirement. For example, a hardware appliance seeking a FIPS 140 level 2 validation must meet the opacity requirement. If the appliance enclosure has ventilation holes that enable a tester (or attacker) to identify the component integrated circuits (IC) inside the module through the ventilation holes, the module would fail the opacity test. However, modifying the ventilation holes or the appliance enclosure to meet the opacity requirement after the product has already been designed and developed can present some engineering challenges such as meeting the opacity requirement while maintaining adequate component cooling. Discovering these inadequacies and making these changes during the FIPS 140 validation process will lead to significant delays and possibly affect product announcement schedules.

Ensuring that the cryptographic module has implemented the appropriate self-tests is key to any type (hardware, software or firmware) module. Self-tests cannot easily be added into the product after the module has been designed and implemented. Even adding software self-tests after the fact would have a significant impact on schedules. These self-tests need to be designed and implemented in the module from the outset.

Track and Manage Customer Expectations

U.S. Federal agencies are required to purchase cryptographic products that have completed FIPS 140 validation or that are officially in the process of pursuing validation. These customers can refer to the NIST CMVP website [CMVL] to find out the latest status for any cryptographic module in the FIPS 140 validation process. Agencies often have disparate requirements for validated products - some require validation on one version of hardware/software, while others require a different version. Some agencies may require overall level 2 validations while others may not have articulated such specific requirements.

While not an easy problem to solve, effectively tracking and managing customer requirements has several benefits. First, a vendor can structure a validation effort that meets the majority of customer needs. Second, such requirements (when coupled with an adequately structured business case) provide a foundation for expediting approvals and commitments from executive management. Finally, building

historical records of customer requirements can help in overall validation strategy development and provides input to product design.

One very important reason to manage customer expectations is
to support sales activities. Oftentimes, the motivation for a FIPS 140
validation is to be able to vie for multi-million dollar government deals
where the customer requires a FIPS 140 validation. Government sales
representatives will report customer requirements for FIPS 140 validations to the product managers. Customers may merely state their
requirement as a FIPS 140 validation, while others may demand the
validation at a specific overall security level. Some customers will
compare competing products and their relative FIPS 140 statuses – in
process or validated and overall security level. Customers, and especially government customers, want to get the most competitive and secure
product they can buy. FIPS 140 validations are one measure of product
quality and security.

Whatever the stated customer requirements are, it is important
to get customers to articulate these requirements as clearly and precisely
as possible. Getting details from the customer helps focus the validation
effort, reduces cost, and saves time.

Once the decision has been made to go forward with the FIPS
140 validation, it is advantageous to communicate this to the customers.
Experience has shown that customers, at least initially, want to see that
the vendors they work with are serious about meeting their requirements. Many times, they are only trying to meet the procurement
regulations (e.g., NSTISSP #11 or FISMA) and just need to know that
their vendors are moving forward. Letters from the vendor to the
customer indicating the plans to engage FIPS 140 testing labs can be an
effective means of demonstrating commitment to meeting customer
requirements. Because of the variability of the FIPS 140 validation
process, it is important to be very careful not to be too specific about
timelines. It is most helpful to also communicate the intent and plan to
move forward to the government sales team so that they can more
readily address other customer inquiries for other contracts.

Identify Internal Champions

Product developers will hire FIPS 140 labs to do the testing and
they may hire FIPS 140 consultants to help develop the necessary
documentation and provide overall project management. These outside
parties will provide technical expertise about FIPS 140, but as with any
project within a commercial product development organization, internal

champions are needed to ensure the project's success. Having internal champions for both technical and program management aspects are ideal.

The program and product management champion will garner executive support to ensure sufficient resources (in terms of both funding and manpower) are applied to the FIPS 140 validation effort. The successful champion will educate all levels of management. Holding strategy discussions with sales representatives and executives help cement the approach to the FIPS 140 validation effort. Periodic status meetings with stakeholders on an on-going basis keep them informed of project progress. Communications with sales representatives and customers is important to manage expectations and improve customer satisfaction. While it is important to meet customer requirements, it is unwise to make detailed (e.g., timeframe) promises because there could be unavoidable or uncontrollable (e.g., NIST) delays to the validation project.

Technical champions can help drive the product development team deliverables and keep the validation project on schedule. The FIPS 140 consultant can define the project schedule and coordinate with the testing lab, but an internal champion is needed to make sure that the product development team is being responsive to inquiries from the FIPS 140 consultant and testing lab.

Successful FIPS 140 validation projects require internal resources that are committed to completing the project. Allocating these resources (both money and people) requires an executive willing and able to champion this effort. Product developers may also benefit from having technical advocates that are able to motivate and direct the technical resources to complete their deliverables during the FIPS 140 validation process. Strong program management also is a key resource to maintain visibility and focus on the deliverables and schedules.

Convincing an executive to allocate and commit the time and money necessary to successfully complete a FIPS 140 validation requires a strong business case. This approval is critical to being able to start, sustain, and complete the FIPS 140 validation project. One of the greatest challenges in preparing for FIPS 140 validation is developing a convincing and compelling business case. In some cases, business executives and product team members immediately recognize the importance of meeting the FIPS 140 validation requirement and are willing to devote the appropriate resources to it. However, in most cases, a more formal business case has to be developed to convince the business leaders to proceed.

There are obviously two major components to developing a return-on-investment (ROI) business case to pursue a FIPS 140 validation. They are:

- Costs (investments)
- Benefits (returns)

Understanding how much the FIPS 140 validation will cost requires a thorough understanding of the requirements, the module cryptographic capabilities, and any vendor evidence gaps. The major cost (i.e., money expense) categories to consider are:

- Evidence development costs
- Validation testing lab costs
- Travel expenses
- NIST cost recovery fees
- Equipment costs

The other half of the ROI analysis is the clear articulation of the benefits of the FIPS 140 validation. It can be difficult to quantify the incremental revenue and other benefits of FIPS 140 validations. In some cases, FIPS 140 validations have proceeded simply because the product manager felt threatened by competitors who had completed FIPS 140 validations or had announced plans to do it.

Often the FIPS 140 validation question arises when a government agency's license contract comes up for renewal and the product developer must demonstrate compliance or plans to comply with the government procurement policy requirements. At that point, there is no upside revenue potential, only the risk of losing the renewal. In the cases where a new customer is seeking a FIPS 140 validated solution, the contract amount is apparent. These new, multi-million dollar opportunities often attract the most management attention and support.

The trick is to develop arguments (quantitative or not) that will support the claims for business benefits to the vendor's company. Researching the FIPS 140 validation status of competitors to highlight potential competitive weaknesses can be useful information in producing convincing arguments. Gathering historical data on lost deals to competitors who had FIPS 140 validated products also can be important information. Projecting incremental revenues based on the pipeline of upcoming contracts from the government that would require FIPS 140 validated products can help illustrate the potential revenue benefits.

Different approaches and different arguments work with different managers, so perhaps the key to success here is to learn what kinds of arguments are most persuasive and use those with the key stakeholders. Some key considerations for developing business cases are:

- What could happen if the FIPS 140 validation proceeds?
- What could happen if the FIPS 140 validation does not proceed?
- What could happen if the FIPS 140 validation is deferred?

Even when using an outside consultant to provide documentation and project management expertise, having an internal advocate is critical to the success of the validation effort. This individual ideally has proven program management experience to drive issue resolution and communication. This resource communicates project status to Federal sales teams and schedules time with software engineers and product managers when appropriate.

Educate All Levels of the Organization

Federal sales, executive management, and project/product managers play a part in the overall certifications strategy, and each one of these entities requires different types and degrees of education. Educated sales staff can better qualify the customers and can more effectively track and manage customer requirements. Educated executive managers can digest the business case, resource allocation, and act more quickly for budgeting and resource approvals. Educated project managers (e.g., the internal advocate) can communicate status and issues to executive management, work to resolve issues quickly, and implement risk/issue mitigation strategies.

Sales representatives meet with customers every day. They are responsible for gathering customer requirements and educating the customers on what products, services, and solutions their company provides. They provide the latest product updates and status information to inform the customer to remain competitive and claim thought leadership. In order for sales representatives to be effective in competing with other companies' offerings, it is important that they have the latest information about the status of FIPS 140 validation efforts. FIPS 140 validation project managers can hold periodic meetings with sales representatives or publish periodic announcements or newsletters highlighting the current status of the FIPS 140 validation efforts. Sales representatives can become more effective in combating competitive announcements by having appropriate tools to demonstrate leadership. FIPS 140 training for them may include an overview of the FIPS 140 validation process and generic timelines will help them understand why the schedule is not deterministic (e.g., NIST backlogs and delayed certifications) and why a validation maintenance program is an important planning tool.

As mentioned earlier, executives need to have a strong business case in order to commit the necessary resources to the FIPS 140 validation project. They also need training on the overall process and the importance of an on-going validation maintenance plan. Customers may have immediate needs, but they will also expect that their providers will anticipate their future needs and establish plans to meet those needs. Executives are responsible for establishing strategic directions and putting in place budget plans. They need to be armed with information about how FIPS 140 validations will enhance the revenue and profits for their product lines.

Project or program managers in charge of shepherding the FIPS 140 validation projects of course need to understand the details of the FIPS 140 preparation and validation process. They need to understand who is responsible for which deliverables and the details of those deliverables. The intent of this book is to give program managers a glimpse into the details of the FIPS 140 process and deliverables. FIPS 140 expert consultants certainly will be able to provide the details specific to the module being submitted for validation and to educate the program managers on their duties during the process.

Develop a Validation Maintenance Program

As products change over time due to the addition of new, state-of-the-art features or to correct defects or mitigate new threats, FIPS 140 validations may need to be renewed. FIPS 140 validation certificates only apply to static module versions and platforms. If there are any changes to the cryptographic module or its surrounding environment, some form of re-validation may be required. NIST periodically updates the FIPS 140 Implementation Guidance [IG] including enhancing guidance on re-validation requirements. Product developers should keep abreast of the re-validation conditions and requirements. FIPS 140 consultants can help provide the latest information concerning this topic and provide recommendations on how to deal with them relative to the specific modules in question. Chapter 14: Issues With FIPS 140 goes into more details of re-validation as explained by the FIPS 140 Implementation Guidance.

Vendors typically have aggressive product development cycles for software releases and bug fixes, and customers generally demand the latest version of software available to maintain a secure environment. Since FIPS 140 validations are specific to hardware and software versions tested, vendors should maintain a validation maintenance program. Of course, validating each hardware/software release may not be feasible or logical, but pursuing re-validations at strategic intervals is a cost-effective way to offer customers a recently released version of code.

Follow Sound Project Management Practices

The FIPS 140 validation is a challenging project. Like any other type of project, following sound project management practices will help ensure that the project completes on-time and on-budget. The FIPS 140 validation project involves coordination with third-parties and coordination with internal teams. The pressure to perform well is heightened by its high-level visibility (mostly because of the revenue-generating potential involved) and sometimes long time span (up to a year). Adhering to strong project management fundamentals will help ensure the success of this. This means having a project manager responsible for:

- Planning – establish the overall evaluation project plan and make real-time adjustments as needed throughout the process
- Monitoring – continuously monitor project progress and identify issues that affect the plan
- Controlling – mitigate issues and update the plan as necessary

Planning

Project planning must be done initially to identify allocated resources, define milestones and deliverables. Project plans will need to be adjusted during the project as changes occur to the plan.

It is important for the FIPS 140 validation project manager to work very closely with the product development team's program manager. The product development program manager is responsible for managing the time for everyone on the engineering and QA teams. Members of the product development team are oftentimes shifted between different projects as priorities and needs change. The program manager ensures that the right personnel and equipment are made available according to the master plan that is developed and maintained by the program manager. The most successful project managers will develop the plan and secure the commitment from all of the participants throughout the life of the project.

From the project outset, it is critical to gain the commitment from the developers and QA team members. A key topic at the initial project kickoff meeting is to discuss the FIPS 140 validation process and everyone's roles and responsibilities within it.

To establish the initial validation project plan, the project manager must develop time estimates for each activity and for everyone involved. An accurate initial plan depends on knowing how much time each person would need to devote to this effort. It is also critical to know when these people will be needed to devote their time to the FIPS 140 validation project in order to determine if there will be any conflicts with other activities (e.g., product releases, Beta test phases). The FIPS 140 validation activities will then be integrated with the time and personnel allocations for the master plan.

Minimizing and managing the scope of the FIPS 140 validation effort will help ensure its successful completion. Having insights into the complexities of the cryptographic module and its development processes can help control the module specification, define the supported platforms, and identify potential issues with the delivery processes. All of this will help establish a solid initial FIPS 140 validation plan.

Monitoring

Monitoring progress against the plan is critical to keeping on track. There are many issues such as new product release efforts and the occasional hot fix patch release that put pressure on vendors. These pressures may impact FIPS 140 validation project activities. It is important to set visible milestones and monitor progress consistently. When using outside consultants to develop and deliver the FIPS 140 test documentation to the testing lab, it is critical to make sure that all parties are synchronized to the same schedule. Weekly project status calls with consultants, the development team, and the testing lab to review progress toward the current set of deliverables and to discuss any issues that might delay deliveries will help to develop contingency plans. Status calls can be used to look ahead at the next set of deliverables and to make sure any dependencies are being addressed. Issues such as making sure the testing lab has an actual product delivered to them for testing should be considered and planned. This may require some coordination with the product manager and should be arranged in advance.

A valuable skill that FIPS 140 consultants can provide is an un-der-standing of the validator's perspective. The consultant that under-stands what the testers need to satisfy their validation requirements will save time in the long run. A good consultant will also recognize that the more easily and clearly the testers can identify the evidence elements they need, the quicker the validation can complete. This can mean developing tables that clearly showed the correlation between evidence documents and the FIPS 140 security requirements.

One of the FIPS 140 project manager's major responsibilities is to make sure that stakeholders understand where the project is in the overall process. Communicating status to the Sales organization is important because customers will ask when the module will meet their procurement requirements. The FIPS 140 validation process can be lengthy (up to a year), so it is important for the sales team and customers to be aware of this. It is equally important for the sales team to know where in the process the project is all along the way. Giving periodic updates to the sales team on the FIPS 140 validation project status is an effective way to keep them up-to-speed. Another useful mechanism is to issue letters to customers announcing the completion of major mile-stones. These open lines of communication can help quell many con-cerns and inquiries from customers and can illustrate the commitment to completing the validations.

Controlling

Reacting to changes "closes the loop" on project management by controlling the resources and deliverables necessary for a successful project completion. Controlling the process is the last step in the project manager's cycle. The successful FIPS 140 validation project manager must drive the product team's responsiveness to inquiries from the testing lab. The product developers are responsible for providing the technical details about the product and the development processes. Delays in responding to the inquiries from FIPS 140 validators can hinder the success of the project.

The effective project manager is adept at controlling the valida-tion process by ensuring that product team members fulfill their respon-sibilities to the project. The strong project manager is also instrumental in making sure that dedicated resources are allocated to develop the necessary vendor evidence for the validation.

A timely completion of any FIPS 140 validation is important to retain credibility with customers and to address competitive concerns. Minimizing rework of the validation evidence is important to reduce the overall time to complete the project. The more time spent on any one piece of evidence, the more time and money that will be spent on the validation. It becomes important to efficiently address any issues and questions that come up during the project. At times it may become necessary to put the developers in direct contact with the testers. This can eliminate any "lost in translation" issues.

Work With Trusted Partners

Proper due diligence practices dictate that as good corporate citizens, decision-makers must establish sound partner selection criteria and use objective, reasoned decision-making processes when hiring outside parties to perform services for the organization. With FIPS 140 validation projects, product developers will employ at least a NIST-accredited FIPS 140 testing laboratory and possibly a FIPS 140 consultant. Selection criteria for both parties should include:

- Demonstrated technical competence (track record)
- Competitive pricing
- Quality of deliverables
- Ease of doing business
- Speed and responsiveness
- Cooperative relationship
- Personnel turnover rates

Naturally, technical competence of any third-party hired to perform tasks is a primary criteria for selection. Technical competence can be demonstrated by the number of successfully, completed projects. The NIST website [CMVL] lists all of the completed FIPS 140 module validations, the product name and type, the manufacturer, key contact information and the validation testing lab. Checking references is another important way to assess technical competence.

Issuing request for quotes (RFQ) to a wide variety of service providers will yield a better understanding for pricing and cost structures. Comparing prices is a corporate obligation to ensure that the company and its shareholders are getting the greatest value for their investments.

Price comparison must go hand-in-hand with quality assessment. Paying a low price for poor quality is not a good investment. Poor quality leads to rework and delays that can affect product releases and market competitiveness. Validation labs that perform their tasks with good quality encounter fewer questions from NIST during their review cycles. FIPS 140 consultants that develop and deliver quality documentation receive fewer questions from the testing lab. Quality is related to technical competence, but quality highlights the excellence of the work performed.

The process for establishing a business relationship can take months. Distributing RFQs, receiving proposals and quotes, creating statements of work (SOW), exchanging confidential disclosure agreements and signing contracts are all necessary legal and financial instruments for conducting business with outside parties. However, delays in this process can result in delays in meeting desired product release and marketing deadlines. Working with cooperative third-parties that make it easy to do business with them is an advantage to the product developer.

Larger organizations may have developed bureaucracies that may be necessary for their operations, but can hinder nimble, speedy responses. Speed and responsiveness are critical competitive differentiators in business today. Companies that can respond quickly to customer requests, whether the customer is a government agency or a product developer, will have a competitive edge.

An intangible, but important characteristic of any third-party is establishing a cooperative relationship with the product developer. Product developers that select FIPS 140 consultants and validation testing labs that can empathize with the developers' constraints and objectives will help ensure a smooth and speedy FIPS 140 validation.

Continuity during the validation process is critical to the success of the project. Changes to personnel during the project can disrupt that continuity and can lead to unacceptable delays. Working with partners who have demonstrated low personnel turnover can help mitigate this risk.

Summary

This chapter has summarized several key time-proven best practices toward successful, timely and cost-effective FIPS 140 cryptographic module validations. These best practices have helped numerous product developers achieve their FIPS 140 validation goals. The best practices are summarized below:

- Consider FIPS 140 requirements at the product design phase
- Track and manage customer expectations
- Identify an internal advocate for the validation project
- Educate all levels of the organization on FIPS 140
- Develop a validation maintenance program
- Follow sound project management practices
- Work with trusted partners

Chapter 15: Issues With FIPS 140

Product developers confront different challenges or issues as they prepare their cryptographic modules for the FIPS 140 validation process. They encounter issues during the testing process as interpretations of the standards are unraveled and reconciled. Product developers developing longer-term validation plans face issues brought on by the evolving standards and changing technologies.

Part 3: Real-World Examples highlighted some of the key issues product developers of specific technology types can expect and how to deal with them. This chapter will discuss some other key issues with the FIPS 140 validation process independent of the product types, but affect the business of pursuing FIPS 140 validations.

Vulnerable or Validated?

The FIPS 140 validation is an examination of a static cryptographic module by accredited, independent third-party testing labs. In this instance, static means that it is assumed that the module under test does not change during the testing process and that the validation is only applicable to that precise, static instance of the module – that is, any changes to the validated module invalidates the certification. The static nature of the FIPS 140 validation is a weakness in the testing scheme as it does not reflect the realities of the modern information technology world where technologies are constantly changing, upgrading, and defending against the latest threats. Government agencies are directed to use only FIPS 140 validated cryptographic modules, so if a validated module is changed after installation, the module is no longer valid and the agency is technically in violation of the regulations. This may force the agency to decide whether to be vulnerable or validated.

Cryptographic modules, especially software-based modules can be upgraded or patched to correct security defects or weaknesses identified after the module has been installed and deployed. Patching is almost an everyday occurrence for many desktop computer systems and updates are provided on a periodic basis from most commercial software vendors. However, FIPS 140 validated cryptographic module providers must think twice before issuing patches for known, disclosed security vulnerabilities in those modules. These patches could invalidate the FIPS 140 module validation.

Even if cryptographic module vendors provide software patches for government end users, the end user may have to decide whether to apply a patch that is intended to correct a known, publicly-disclosed security flaw or leave the module alone to maintain its validated status. From a practical standpoint, agencies will make local decisions on what makes the most sense to them and their circumstances, but the situation raises a question worth considering: How could the FIPS 140 crypto-graphic module validation scheme be modified to address the realities of software patching? Answering this question is beyond the scope of this book, but security experts and business leaders perhaps should ponder this issue.

An option that is available today is module re-validation. Re-validation is discussed later in this chapter. While re-validation is only a partial solution, it does provide some relief to resolving this issue of vulnerable or validated.

FIPS 140 Compliance and FIPS 140 Validation

NSTISSP #11 and other formal regulations and NIST statements concerning the use of FIPS 140 validated modules have been established in the interest of providing a level of assurance that the cryptographic technologies used by the government and others have been examined against well-established standards. These statements have said that modules that implement cryptographic functions must be FIPS 140 validated.

The concept of "FIPS 140 compliant" emerged as commercial cryptographic module providers sold or licensed FIPS 140 validated modules to other product developers so that those developers could integrate the validated modules into their applications and systems. These applications and systems have met the spirit of NSTISSP #11 and the other government regulations by using cryptographic modules that have been FIPS 140 validated even though the cryptographic module was not developed by the application developer.

NIST has tried to emphasize the fact that a FIPS 140 compliant application or system meets the spirit of the regulation as long as the application integrating the validated module uses it in accordance to the instructions in the module's Security Policy. Technically, the application is as secure as if the application developer took the very same module through the FIPS 140 validation process themselves.

The issue arises when customers and competitors make it seem that FIPS 140 complaint is somehow not as worthy or secure as FIPS 140

174

validated. Some customers have insisted that they will only purchase and use applications or systems that have FIPS 140 validated modules with the application developer's name on it. Some vendors have marketed the fact that the cryptographic modules that are used within their products were validated by them and imply that products that are just FIPS 140 compliant are somehow inferior or less secure.

Common Criteria

The Common Criteria for Information Technology Security Evaluation (CC) is an international standard for evaluating information security products. Product vendors can make security functional claims about their products and evaluate then against evaluation assurance claims. The CC standards include elements related to the use of cryptographic technologies. There has been some confusion amongst customers and vendors alike over the differences between these two important security evaluation regimes. There is confusion because both are mentioned in NSTISSP #11 and both are security evaluation schemes. Comparisons and possible synergies between FIPS 140 validations and CC evaluations have been publicly discussed as recently as the 2010 International Common Criteria Conference [ICCC] in Turkey.

Dawn Adams and Erin Connor of EWA-Canada, a FIPS 140 and CC testing laboratory, presented a study [Adams] at the conference in Turkey of the comparison between FIPS 140 requirements and comparable requirements in CC. They concluded that the CC evaluation of cryptographic functions replicates and in some cases is inferior to FIPS 140 testing. They also pointed out that the FIPS 140 validation effort produces significant evidence and test results that could be reused in a CC evaluation.

CC has a functional security class called Cryptographic Support, which pertains to topics common to FIPS 140. The Cryptographic Support class (FCS) has two families of requirements: cryptographic key management (FCS_CKM) and cryptographic operation (FCS_COP).

FCS_CKM contains requirements for key generation, distribution, access, and destruction. These align well with some of the security requirements described in Section 4.7: Cryptographic Key Management of the FIPS 140 standard.

FCS_COP describes the cryptographic algorithms used by the target of evaluation (TOE). FIPS 140 goes further with this notion and requires the algorithms to be tested under the Cryptographic Algorithm Validation Program (CAVP).

175

The EWA-Canada study also points out that there are several "logistics tail" security functional requirements (SFR) associated with the FCS_CKM and FCS_COP requirements. Logistics tail SFRs are security requirements upon which FCS_CKM and FCS_COP requirements are dependent. This means that there are several more CC SFRs that are introduced when dealing with the FCS cryptographic requirements.

There have been recent discussions that new CC protection profiles that define security requirements for specific technology types will incorporate more requirements for cryptographic functions. This should precipitate further discussions about the leverage and synergy between FIPS 140 validations and CC evaluations. As the EWA-Canada study indicates, there is an opportunity for reuse of FIPS 140 validation results for CC evaluations.

Re-Validation

FIPS 140 module re-validations are not an issue per se but situations have arisen that required the FIPS 140 Implementation Guidance [IG] to be updated to provide instruction on how to deal with these different circumstances. Previously validated cryptographic modules may change over time or new modules based significantly on previously validated modules seeking FIPS 140 validation are situations covered by the Implementation Guidance (IG) document. Section G.8 of the FIPS 140 IG deals specifically with the conditions under which module re-validations are required and the responsibilities of the vendor and testing lab in each instance. In some cases, full module re-validation is not required, but some kind of assessment of the past validation and the module changes is required. The five situations discussed in IG Section G.8 are:

1. No security-relevant changes to a previously validated module
2. Additonal security-relevant features are claimed
3. Less than 30% security-relevant changes are made
4. Physical boundary change only
5. New cryptographic module

No Security-Relevant Changes

When modifications are made to hardware, software or firmware components that do not affect any FIPS 140 security relevant items of a previously validated module, the vendor provides applicable documentation identifying these modifications to the FIPS 140 testing laboratory. The documentation will include the previous validation report, design documentation, and source code. The testing laboratory reviews the vendor-supplied documentation and will decide on any additional testing needed to confirm that the modifications have not affected any FIPS 140 security relevant items. When the testing lab has successfully completed its review and testing, the lab shall submit a signed explanatory letter to NIST. The letter will contain a description of the modifications, a list of the affected derived test requirements, and the lab assessment. The lab assessment shall include the analysis performed by the laboratory that confirms that no security relevant items were affected. The letter will also indicate whether the modified cryptographic module replaces the previously validated module or adds to the latter.

Additional Security Features Claimed

For previously validated FIPS 140 cryptographic modules that want to claim additional security features, the FIPS 140 testing lab is responsible for identifying the necessary documentation required of the vendor. Under this scenario, no changes to the module hardware, software or firmware components or version information are allowed. This situation arises when testing was not available for the additional security relevant function at the time of the original validation or the additional security relevant functions were not tested during the original validation.

The FIPS 140 testing lab is responsible for identifying the documentation that is needed to determine whether a re-validation is sufficient and the vendor is responsible for submitting the requested documentation to the lab. Documentation may include a previous validation report and applicable NIST rulings, design documentation, and source code. The testing lab shall identify the security assertions affected and performs the appropriate tests.

The testing lab will then submit a test report describing the assertions that have been newly tested to NIST. If new algorithm certificates were obtained, they shall be listed. A new certificate will not be issued.

Less Than 30% Security-Relevant Changes

The FIPS 140 testing lab is responsible for identifying the appropriate documentation needed when vendors make minor modifications to validated modules' hardware, software and/or firmware. Changes to these components may affect some of the FIPS 140-2 security items. FIPS 140 validated modules with only minor changes to the security policy and finite state model and changes to less than 30% of the modules security features are considered in this scenario.

The FIPS 140 testing lab may require from the vendor the previous validation report, applicable NIST rulings, module design documentation, and source code. The testing then identifies the security assertions affected by the modifications and performs the associated tests.

The FIPS 140 testing laboratory must provide a summary of the changes and rationale of how the less than 30% guideline is met. The testing lab shall document the test results and submit a test report to NIST. Upon a satisfactory review by NIST, the updated version will be re-validated and a new certificate will be issued.

Physical Boundary Changes Only

In the situation where modifications are made only to the physical enclosure of the cryptographic module and there are no operational changes to the module, the FIPS 140 testing lab is responsible for verifying that the changes only affect the physical integrity and has no operational impact on the module. The testing lab must also fully test the physical security features of the new enclosure to ensure its compliance to the relevant requirements of the standard. The testing lab then submits a letter to NIST that describes the changes and provides information supporting the claims that there has been no operational impact.

The letter also will describe the tests performed by the lab that confirm that the modified enclosure still provides the same physical protection attributes as the previously validated module. An updated Physical Security Test Report will be submitted for security levels 2, 3 and 4.

An example of such a change under this scenario would be the plastic enclosure of a FIPS 140 Physical Security level 2 token, which has been reformulated or colored. This change is security relevant as the encapsulation meets opacity and tamper evidence requirements. This can be handled as a letter only change with evidence that the new

178

composition has the same physical security relevant attributes as the prior composition.

New Cryptographic Module

Any modifications to hardware, software, or firmware components of a previously FIPS 140 validated module that do not meet the previous four scenarios is considered a new module and must undergo a full validation testing by a FIPS 140 validation lab. Also, if the overall security level of the cryptographic module changes or if the physical embodiment changes (e.g., from multi-chip standalone to multi-chip embedded), then the cryptographic module will be considered a new module and must undergo full validation testing.

Keeping Up With New Technologies

The FIPS 140 validation program was established in 1994 before software was prevalent and certainly before the increased interest in open source software. The FIPS 140 standards, policies and guidance have been updated in an attempt to keep up with technology trends, but issues still remain. Some of these issues are focused on the physical security requirements of the FIPS 140 validation scheme.

Some of the key issues faced by hardware appliance vendors were raised in Chapter 9: Hardware Appliance. In particular, the physical security requirement for opacity seems to cause many vendors to spend an inordinate amount of effort to design their products specifically to meet this requirement. The original reason for the opacity requirement was to counter the threat that attackers might gain insights into how to subvert the cryptographic module by identifying components within the module. With the design of today's integrated circuits and the use of stock commercial components, the availability of component information on the Internet (and elsewhere), and the use of software and firmware to yield the cryptographic functionality, the likelihood that attackers would glean any useful information by shining a flashlight into an appliance's case is remote. The opacity requirement for many products seems superfluous.

Chapter 10: Security Software Application and Chapter 11: Data Encryption Library pointed out some of the challenges vendors of these product types can expect when pursuing FIPS 140 validations. Operational Environment and EMI/EMC requirements are at the heart of the issues faced by software modules seeking overall level 2 validations. Software cryptographic modules claim that the hardware computer platform upon which the software is running will satisfy the Operational Environment and EMI/EMC requirements even though the hardware is not within the cryptographic boundary. For software modules, the FIPS 140 Physical Security requirements are considered "not applicable", but referring to the computer hardware test platforms seems contrary to the definition of what is being tested and validated.

As new technologies continue to evolve and appear, FIPS 140 standards and guidance needs to be relevant, realistic and effective in ensuring that customers gain a sufficient level of confidence in the cryptographic modules they purchase and use. Appropriate validations for open source software and cloud computing are needed so that customers can have confidence in using these attractive technologies.

Summary

Customers may be faced with the situation of deciding to patch their cryptographic module to fix a security vulnerability at the risk of invalidating the module's FIPS 140 certification. While this issue is not a FIPS 140 standards issue, it does affect the consumers of the validated modules and calls into question the rationality of the policies around FIPS 140.

Customers and competitors have used FIPS 140 compliance and FIPS 140 validation as differentiators and yet realistically both meet the objectives of providing end-users with cryptographic functionality that has been reviewed against agreed-upon standards and testing criteria. In spite of NIST's attempts to educate customers, the notion persists that FIPS 140 validation is somehow better or more secure than FIPS 140 compliance.

There continues to be confusion about the differences between the Common Criteria and FIPS 140 certifications. There are opportunities for greater synergy between these two testing regimes that can save vendors and customers time and effort by reducing duplicated testing.

The FIPS 140 Implementation Guidance has detailed the scenarios under which cryptographic module re-validation is required. For the most part, the FIPS 140 testing lab is charged with determining how much additional documentation and testing will be needed to validate a modified module.

Physical security requirements raise some questions for both hardware and software module vendors. The requirements sometimes seem unrealistic given the extensive use of modern technologies. This may be an area for future examination to help FIPS 140 remain relevant and valuable to end users.

Chapter 16: Future of FIPS 140

The immediate future of FIPS 140 is defined in FIPS 140-3, the upcoming revision to the cryptographic module validation standards and NIST Special Publication 800-131 [SP 800-131] that details the latest revisions to the cryptographic algorithm standards. NIST is required by Federal regulation to review and update the FIPS standards every 5 years, but technologies also change and the applicable standards must be updated to maintain the integrity and security of systems using cryptographic modules.

FIPS 140-3

FIPS 140-3 is the next planned revision of the FIPS 140 standard. This version has been discussed since 2004. There has been significant anticipation about the timing of the release of FIPS 140-3. Some initial plans presented by NIST in 2004 indicated they had planned to have FIPS 140-3 ready for use by 2006, but now it appears that it will not be ready until 2011 at the earliest. At the time of this writing, the public comment period for the second draft have all been received and are being incorporated into a package to be presented to the U.S. Department of Commerce for approval. After that, the updated Derived Test Requirements (DTR) and Implementation Guidance (IG) will be published, and then testing using FIPS 140-3 will be ready to begin. Figure 46 summarizes the timeline of events related to the FIPS 140-3 development.

Date	Activity
TBD	FIPS 140-2 ends
TBD	FIPS 140-3 testing begins
TBD	DTR and IG released
1Q 2011	FIPS 140-3 presented to Dept. of Commerce
4Q 2010	Prepare FIPS 140-3 for Dept. of Commerce
Oct. 2010	Process all comments
May 2010	End public comment period
Dec 2009	Second public draft
July 2007	First public draft

Figure 46: FIPS 140-3 Timeline

Product developers have been keenly interested in the timing of the release of FIPS 140-3 because they want to be able to plan for any changes to the testing criteria. They are concerned because they need to allocate the necessary development time and resources to commit to meet the requirements and then time the release of the product appropriately. Fortunately, NIST is aware of the need for vendors to have a transition period from FIPS 140-2 to FIPS 140-3. Figure 47 shows how NIST will allow a time where FIPS 140-2 validation will continue to be performed after the initial release of FIPS 140-3 testing. This same approach was taken with the FIPS 140-1 to FIPS 140-2 transition in 2001 with a transition period of about 6 months. For some product developers, 6 months may be a challenge to make the transition which enhances the need to keep abreast of the latest announcements by NIST and to review the available draft standards and guidance.

The transition time along with public releases of draft standards give product developers an opportunity to see what kinds of changes are being planned for the next version of FIPS 140. The difficulty is the anticipation and waiting for the final version to be published. Perhaps more important are the updated Derived Test Requirements (DTR) and Implementation Guidance (IG) because these documents contain the intimate details of the module feature, vendor evidence and testing requirements.

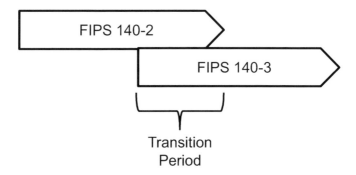

Figure 47: Transition

The second revision of FIPS 140-3 was released in December 2009 and was open to public comment until March 2010. Based on the information from second draft, a review of the FIPS 140-3 draft was presented at the 2010 International Common Criteria Conference [ICCC].

This review highlighted the changes from FIPS 140-2 including the new security categories shown in Figure 48 which identify the new category names in **bold face type**.

FIPS 140-2	FIPS 140-3
Cryptographic module specification	Cryptographic module specification
Cryptographic module ports and interfaces	**Cryptographic module interfaces**
Roles, services, and authentication	Roles, authentication, and services
Finite state model	**Software/firmware security**
Physical security	Physical security
Cryptographic key management	**Physical security – non-invasive attacks**
EMI/EMC	**Sensitive security parameter mgmt.**
Self-tests	Self-tests
Design assurance	**Life-cycle assurance**
Operational environment	Operational environment
Mitigation of other attacks	Mitigation of other attacks

Figure 48: FIPS 140-3 Security Categories

Some of the other key changes that appeared in the FIPS 140-3 second draft are:

- Introduces the notion of firmware cryptographic module and defines the security requirements for it
- Limits the overall security level for software cryptographic modules to security level 2
- Includes requirements for mitigation of non-invasive attacks at higher security levels
- Eliminates the requirement for formal modeling at security level 4
- Modifies conditions for pre-operational/power-up self-tests, and strengthened integrity testing
- Removes all Common Criteria requirements from Operational Environment requirements

All of the above comments reflect the contents of the second public draft of FIPS 140-3 and do not contain any of the comments from the draft. At the time of this writing, NIST is in the process of examining and processing the public comments and preparing a presentation to the U.S. Department of Commerce. It is not until the Department of Commerce approves the new standard and when NIST publishes the associated Derived Test Requirements and Implementation Guidance, can real conclusions be drawn about the impact of the new standards on cryptographic modules.

SP 800-131A

The National Institute of Standards and Technology (NIST) began providing cryptographic key management guidance to define and implement appropriate key management procedures using solid algorithms. NIST Special Publication 800-57, Part 1 [SP 800-57] on key management includes a general approach for transitioning from one algorithm or key length to another. NIST SP 800-131A [SP 800-131A] provides more specific guidance for transitions to stronger, updated cryptographic keys and algorithms. The algorithms covered in NIST SP 800-131A includes:

- Encryption
- Digital Signatures
- Random Number Generation
- Key Agreement Using Diffie-Hellman and Menezes–Qu–Vanstone
- Key Agreement and Key Transport Using RSA
- Key Wrapping
- Deriving Additional Keys from a Cryptographic Key
- Hash Functions
- Message Authentication Codes

SP 800-131A specifies the updated list of acceptable and restricted use algorithms as well as a transition timeline. The publication also details key length requirement changes and transitions.

Other Standards

The draft NIST SP 800-131A document published in January 2011 provided some information on plans for upcoming new standard publications that would affect the FIPS 140 validation program. SP 800-135, Recommendation for Existing Application-Specific Key Derivation Functions and SP 800-133, Recommendation for Cryptographic Key Generation are under development. Also, a draft of a key wrapping mode for block ciphers is currently being prepared. This document will include the AES key wrap specification.

Chapter 17: Wrap-Up

Cryptographic technologies have been protecting important data for centuries. It is still one of the foundational technologies used in information security today. Preventing unauthorized access to confidential information is an important consideration for public and private sector enterprises as well as consumers. Equally important is the confidence users have in the cryptographic technologies they purchase and use. Users can gain confidence in these cryptographic modules if they successfully pass testing against internationally-recognized standards. FIPS 140 is a prescriptive set of security requirements for the design, implementation, delivery, installation, configuration, and use of hardware, software, and firmware cryptographic modules. The U.S. government and other entities around the world require or recommend that their users purchase and use cryptographic modules that have been FIPS 140 validated. These requirements provide a strong financial motivation to product developers on top of the motivation to deliver secure products to their customers.

The FIPS 140 validation process can be daunting and confusing to the uninitiated. The purpose of this book is to give the reader an overview of the requirements, the validation process, and some best practices. The goal is to prepare the product developer for successfully completing the FIPS 140 validation efficiently and cost-effectively while meeting expected time schedules.

Validation Process

The successful FIPS 140 validation process actually begins with the design of the cryptographic module. Figure 49 depicts an overall view of the major phases of the FIPS 140 validation process starting with the Implement phase which incorporates the module design work. Many FIPS 140 security requirements can only be addressed if the requirements are designed into the module and not "bolted on." Physical security requirements such as opaque enclosures and tamper-evident seals need to be considered in the original design of the hardware modules. Implementing only FIPS 140-approved cryptographic algorithms naturally are required, but the associated power-up and conditional self-tests must also be implemented.

The next step is the evidence documentation phase. With the help of FIPS 140 consultants, product developers can quickly and efficiently define and develop the necessary documents for submission to the testing lab. Assembling and developing the right set of documents helps ensure a smooth and cost-effective testing process. The documentation must reflect the realities of the cryptographic module development and operation. The best documentation will make it easy for the testing lab personnel to do their job.

Figure 49: Phases

Once the evidence documentation has been prepared, it is submitted to the NIST-accredited FIPS 140 validation testing lab. The Derived Testing Requirements (DTR) document drives the testing activities of the lab as they assess the cryptographic module against the FIPS 140 security requirements. When the testing lab personnel complete their testing, they produce a report and submit a package to NIST.

NIST reviews the test results and other documentation submitted by the testing lab. NIST may have queries that can be addressed by the testing lab and on occasion, may require a response from the product developers. Once all of the questions have been addressed, NIST will validate the results, issue a FIPS 140 certificate, and post the public Security Policy document on the NIST website.

Deliverables

The key concerns for the product developer in the FIPS 140 validation process is: 1) make sure the cryptographic module has all of the necessary security features and; 2) produce the proper set of documents to be submitted to the testing lab. The documents must support the claims made about the cryptographic module relative to the FIPS 140 security requirements. There are 3 key documents that must be submitted to the FIPS 140 testing lab along with the cryptographic module and some supporting documentation. The 3 main documents are:

- Security Policy
- Finite State Model
- Vendor Evidence

Security Policy

The Security Policy document provides an introduction to the cryptographic module and a high-level summary of how the module meets FIPS 140 security requirements. Since many modules require special configuration to meet FIPS 140 requirements, the Security Policy also provides instructions on how to initialize and operate the module in the FIPS 140-approved mode of operation. This document is non-proprietary and is posted on the NIST website with the module's validation certificate. The Security Policy contains the following policies:

- Identification and Authentication
- Access Control
- Physical Security
- Mitigation of Other Attacks

The Security Policy also contains the Crypto Officer and User Guidance that provides information to the users on how to install, configure and operate the cryptographic module in the secure, FIPS 140-approved mode.

Finite State Model

The Finite State Model depicts the cryptographic module's states and transitions and augments the vendor evidence that addresses the requirements in Section 4 of the Derived Test Requirements. This document also addresses services available in each state. The Finite State Model is represented as a graph of states (usually depicted as bubbles), transitions (depicted as directed arcs), and labels describing the states and transitions. A table also is used to explain the transitions from one state to another.

Vendor Evidence

The Vendor Evidence document addresses Derived Test Re-quirements (DTR) and provides a basis of input for the report from the testing laboratory. This document provides detailed descriptions of how the module meets each applicable requirement in each applicable section of FIPS 140. The security categories identified in the DTR and addressed in the Vendor Evidence document are:

1. Cryptographic Module Specification
2. Cryptographic Module Ports and Interfaces
3. Roles, Services, and Authentication
4. Finite State Model
5. Physical Security
6. Operational Environment
7. Cryptographic Key Management
8. EMI/EMC
9. Self-Tests
10. Design Assurance
11. Mitigation of Other Attacks

The specific security requirements within each category that must be addressed depend upon the security level sought. There are four security levels that are applied to each of the 11 categories. An overall security level is assigned based on the lowest level of the categories. That is, the cryptographic module and the submitted documentation are evaluated against the security requirements of each category and assessed a level. The lowest level is the assigned overall level of the module. The overall level and the levels of the individual categories are reported in the Security Policy, the FIPS 140 certificate, and on the NIST website.

Supporting Vendor Documents

The formal documents that must be submitted to the FIPS 140 testing lab are the Security Policy, Finite State Model, and Vendor Evidence document. Supporting vendor documents must also be provided to the testing lab to fully justify the security claims made about the cryptographic module. These supporting documents can include:

*   EMI/EMC certificates
*   Configuration Management Plan
*   Delivery and Operation documentation
*   Development documentation

A key to successfully completing the FIPS 140 validation as scheduled and within budget is the ability to respond quickly to consultant, testing lab, and NIST questions. The FIPS 140 validation process contains a number of submit-review-query-response-finalize loops where documents are submitted and reviewed. During the review, questions arise and a timely response can help avoid delays in finalizing the documents and completing the validation.

Costs and Timelines

Throughout this book, it has been emphasized that product developers should seek to successfully complete the FIPS 140 validations as quickly and cost-effectively as possible. An important part of accomplishing this goal is anticipating and managing costs. Following sound due diligence practices is an important business management tool toward managing costs. Soliciting quotes from a wide variety of experienced, competent, and cooperative FIPS 140 consultants and testing laboratories will provide valuable information toward making informed selections.

Fixed-price contracts from consultants and testing labs is preferred over time and materials (T&M) contracts because they provide the right incentives for both parties to complete the validation effort quickly and cost-effectively.

Managing project scope be constraining the cryptographic boundary and the security functions claimed will minimize the risk to the validation effort. Focusing attention on customer-valued features will help maximize the return on the validation investment. The product developer has to balance customer requirements against competitive pressures and resource availability to arrive at the optimal approach.

FIPS 140 validation lab testing costs vary depending on the scope and complexity of the cryptographic module, the security level, and the overhead costs of the testing lab organization. Table 23 provides some estimated example lab costs for level 1 and 2 testing.

Overall Level	Estimated Lab Costs
Level 1	$20,000 - 35,000
Level 2	$30,000 - 45,000

Table 23: Lab Costs

In addition to the fees paid to the testing lab, NIST charges a "cost recovery" fee to product developers for the validation services they provide. Table 24 summarizes the NIST fees that vary depending on the security level of the validation.

Overall Level	NIST Fees
Level 1	$2,750
Level 2	$3,750
Level 3	$5,250
Level 4	$7,250

Table 24: NIST Fees

FIPS 140 validations can take 8 to 13 months from the time documentation preparation begins until the NIST validation and certification is complete. Table 25 summarizes the estimated durations of each phase in the FIPS 140 validation process.

Phase	Duration
Documentation	1 - 3 months
Testing	3 – 5 months
Validation	3 – 5 months
Total	7 – 13 months

Table 25: Timeline

Armed with these cost and time estimates, product developers can allocate the appropriate resources and work the validation effort into the overall product roadmap plans.

Best Practices

From the experience gained from several FIPS 140 validation projects, some practices have emerged that have proven to be effective in reducing costs and effort to complete these validation projects. These practices are useful in many other project types, but are particularly useful for FIPS 140 validation projects because they address the need to design in the necessary security features, gain sponsorship from a project champion, and work cooperatively with outside parties. The best practices covered in the book are:

- Consider FIPS 140 requirements at the product design phase
- Track and manage customer expectations
- Identify an internal advocate for the validation project
- Educate all levels of the organization on FIPS 140
- Develop a validation maintenance program
- Follow sound project management practices
- Work with trusted partners

Real-World Examples

Part 3 of this book covered real-world examples of past FIPS 140 validation projects. These chapters covered different product and module types and the unique circumstances they faced during their FIPS 140 validations. These chapters covered the following product/module types:

- Hardware Appliance
- Security Software Application
- Data Encryption Library
- USB Flash Drive
- Open Source Library

In Closing

FIPS 140 Demystified: An Introductory Guide for Developers provides developers a clear, concise description of the FIPS 140 standards, validation process, and some of its nuances. The descriptions are for those readers who may not have or want to have an intimate knowledge of the FIPS 140 standards, but need to understand what it takes to complete the process in order to remain competitive.

This book highlights the special considerations for the different module types and the issues product developers can expect.

GLOSSARY OF TERMS AND ABBREVIATIONS

Accreditation
FIPS 140 labs are accredited by national government agencies to conduct FIPS 140 validations. Accreditation involves meeting quality process standards and demonstrated expertise in FIPS 140 evaluations.

Architecture
Module architecture refers to the high-level structure and design of the product including its major modules and interfaces. The Architecture may also include specific technologies used in the module.

Assurance
Assurance is confidence that the Target of Evaluation (TOE) or product will operate securely. Assurance is gained by independent, third-party evaluation against internationally-recognized security standards.

Best Practices
Practices become known as Best Practices when they have proven to be particularly effective. Best Practices have been demonstrated to be effective in a number of circumstances and environments.

Buy Versus Build
Buy versus Build decisions are made to determine whether it is better to purchase outsourced services or products over using in-house resources to perform the service or deliver the product. The Buy-versus-Build analysis requires consideration of several factors including costs and benefits.

Certification
Certification (or validation) marks the final, official completion of a successful FIPS 140 validation.

Ciphertext
Ciphertext or encrypted text is the result of encrypting plaintext using a cryptographic algorithm.

Configuration
Configuration refers to the settings or customization of products for use in customer environments. These configuration settings adjust for the unique deployment environment. Inappropriate security settings may result in exploitable vulnerabilities.

Configuration Management
Product configuration management (CM) controls and organizes the components of the product to ensure that all of the correct component versions are used to build the product. For software products, configuration management is usually managed by source code control tools such as CVS or Perforce.

Critical Security Parameter
Critical security parameters are security-related information such as secret and private cryptographic keys, and authentication data such as passwords. The disclosure or modification of critical security parameters can compromise the security of a cryptographic module.

Cryptographic Boundary
The cryptographic boundary is the well-defined perimeter that establishes the physical bounds of a cryptographic module and contains all the hardware, software, and/or firmware components of a cryptographic module.

Cryptographic Module
Cryptographic module is a product or part of a product that encapsulates some cryptographic technology.

Cryptographic or Encryption Technology
Cryptographic or encryption technology is the embodiment of the encryption process as in the form of hardware or software.

Cryptography

Cryptography (or cryptology) is defined as the practice and study of hiding information.

Defense in Depth

Defense in depth is the concept of employing several layers of information security measures to protect information assets.

Digital Signature

Digital signature is the result of a cryptographic transformation of data which provides origin authentication, data integrity, and signer non-repudiation.

Due Diligence

Due diligence is the practice of carefully examining alternatives before committing to purchase. Vendors will practice due diligence prior to selecting evaluation labs or consultants. This examination will include assessments across a variety of categories including: price, technical expertise, demonstrated experience and quality.

Encryption

Encryption (or encoding) is the process of transforming information into a form that is understandable only to those for which the information is intended.

Environmental Failure Protection

Environmental failure protection is the use of features to protect against a compromise of the security of a cryptographic module due to environmental conditions or fluctuations such as heat outside of the module's normal operating range.

Environmental Failure Test

Environmental failure test is the use of testing to provide assurance that the security of a cryptographic module will not be compromised by environmental conditions or fluctuations outside of the module's normal operating range.

Error Detection Code

Error detection code is a code computed from data and comprised of redundant bits of information designed to detect unintentional changes in the data.

Evaluation

Evaluation is the examination of evidence by independent, accredited third-party testing laboratories. Independent examination against international standards is the foundation for the Common Criteria (CC). Security assurance is derived through evaluation.

Federal Information Processing Standard 140

Federal Information Processing Standard 140 (FIPS 140) is the standard maintained by the U.S. National Institute of Standards and Technology (NIST) and the Canadian Communications Security Establishment (CSE) pertaining to cryptographic module standards.

Finite State Model

A finite state model is a mathematical model of a system that is comprised of a finite set of input events, output events, and states. The FSM also maps states' inputs to outputs, state transitions, and describes the initial state.

Fixed-Price

Fixed-price contracts are financial agreements between service providers and clients whereby the client agrees to pay a firm, fixed-price for services and deliverables provided by the vendor.

Hash

A hashing procedure transforms a large block of data into a single value (hash value) such that any changes to the data will change the hash value.

Implementation Under Test

The implementation under test is the term used by NIST and FIPS 140 testing labs to designate the cryptographic module submitted to FIPS 140 validation testing.

Information Technology

Information Technology (IT) is the general term used for computers, electronic data storage, networking, operating systems, databases, application software and other technologies used to process, transmit, and store electronic information.

Intellectual Property
Intellectual Property (IP) is the knowledge or technology owned by an organization. IP generally has some competitive value and must be protected in order to maintain a competitive advantage in the marketplace.

Key Establishment
Key establishment is the process by which cryptographic keys are securely distributed among cryptographic modules using a combination of manual and/or automated transport methods.

Key Generation
Key generation is the act of creating cryptographic keys. These keys are used to encrypt plaintext to ciphertext and to decrypt ciphertext to plaintext.

Key Management
Key management arc the activities involving the handling of cryptographic keys and other related security parameters during the entire life cycle of the keys, including their generation, storage, establishment, entry and output, and zeroization.

Known Answer Tests
Known answer tests are functional tests of cryptographic algorithms to check for the proper operation of the cryptographic functions using previously generated results from selected inputs.

Non-repudiation
Non-repudiation is the concept that the integrity and origin of data can be proven with authentication.

Personally Identifiable Information
Personally identifiable information is information that is used to uniquely identify an individual. This information is commonly used for authentication purpose.

Plaintext
Plaintext is human-readable and natural language text.

Platforms
Platforms refer to the computing base upon which application software will execute. The Platform may be viewed as the dependencies of the application software including: operating system, computer hardware and networking.

Private Key
A private key is a cryptographic key, used in conjunction with a public key cryptographic algorithm that is uniquely associated with an entity and is not made public.

Public Key
A public key is a cryptographic key used with a public key cryptographic algorithm that is uniquely associated with an entity and that may be made public.

Quality Assurance
Quality Assurance (QA) is a function within the developer organization chartered with the responsibility for establishing and executing product quality practices. The QA team is usually responsible for developing and executing product tests.

Secure Development
Secure Development is the set of practices believed to result in a more secure product. These practices may include: security training, use of security tools, security testing and use of secure coding practices.

Security Policy
The cryptographic module security policy is a precise specification of the security rules under which a cryptographic module will operate, including the rules derived from the requirements of the FIPS 140 standard and additional rules imposed by the vendor.

Split Knowledge
Split knowledge is the process by which a cryptographic key is split into multiple components. Individually each component is insufficient to encrypt or decrypt data, but can be re-assembled to recreate the original cryptographic key.

Tamper Detection
Tamper detection is the automatic determination by a cryptographic module that an attempt has been made to compromise the physical security of the module.

Tamper Evidence
Tamper evidence is the external indication that an attempt has been made to compromise the physical security of a cryptographic module.

Tamper Response
Tamper response is the automatic action taken by a cryptographic module when tamper detection has occurred.

Time and Materials
Time and Materials (T&M) contracts are set up whereby the provider is paid based on the time and materials actually spend on a project. The customer only pays for what has been used. Fixed-price contracts are an alternative.

Time-to-Market
Time-to-Market (TTM) is the concept that products that are introduced into the marketplace ahead of the competition enjoy a revenue generation advantage. TTM drives product vendors to try to be first on the market with a new product or new capability.

Validation
Validation is the process of testing and verifying that a cryptographic module meets the security requirements claimed in the cryptographic security policy.

Version
A version is a uniquely identifiable variation or revision of a product. Common Criteria evaluations are valid only for a specified version of a product. That version is specified in the Security Target document.

Vulnerabilities
Vulnerabilities are security flaws or weaknesses that may be accidentally or maliciously exploited to expose unauthorized access to data or systems.

Zeroization

Zeroization is a method of erasing electronically stored data, cryptographic keys, and CSPs by altering or deleting the contents of the data storage to prevent recovery of the data.

Abbreviations

AES	Advanced Encryption Standard
ANSI	American National Standards Institute
API	Application Programmatic Interface
ASIC	Application-Specific Integrated Circuit
AV	Anti-Virus
B2B	Business-to-Business
B2C	Business-to-Customer
CAI	Common Air Interface
CAPP	Controlled Access Protection Profile
CAVP	Cryptographic Algorithm Validation Program
CBC	Cipher Block Chaining
CC	Common Criteria
CCM	Counter with Cipher Block Chaining-Message Authentication Code
CD-ROM	Compact Disc – Read-Only Memory
CFR	Code of Federal Regulations
CM	Configuration Management
CMAC	Cipher Block Chaining Mode Authentication Code
CMVP	Cryptographic Module Validation Program
CSEC	Communications Security Establishment of Canada
CSP	Critical Security Parameter
CST	Cryptographic and Security Testing
CTO	Communications Tasking Order
DAC	Discretionary Access Control
DES	Data Encryption Standard
DISA	Defense Information Systems Agency
DOD	Department of Defense
DPA	Differential Power Analysis
DRBG	Deterministic Random Bit Generator
DSA	Digital Signature Algorithm
DSS	Digital Signature Standard
DTR	Derived Test Requirements
EAL	Evaluation Assurance Level
ECB	Electronic Codebook
ECDSA	Elliptic Curve Digital Signature Algorithm
EDC	Error Detection Code

EES	Escrowed Encryption Standard
EFP	Environmental Failure Protection
EFT	Environmental Failure Test
EMC	Electro-Magnetic Compatibility
EMI	Electro-Magnetic Interference
FCC	Federal Communications Commission
FCS	Cryptographic Support class
FCS_CKM	Cryptographic Key Management
FCS_COP	Cryptographic Operation
FIPS	Federal Information Processing Standard
FISMA	Federal Information Security Management Act
FSM	Finite State Model
FSP	Functional Specifications
GCM	Galois/Counter Mode
GPC	General Purpose Computer
GUI	Graphical User Interface
HDL	Hardware Description Language
HMAC	Hashed Message Authentication Code
HTTP	Hypertext Transport Protocol
HTTPS	Hypertext Transport Protocol - Secure
IAAPL	Information Assurance Approved Products List
IC	Integrated Circuit
IG	Implementation Guidance
IPSec	Internet Protocol Security
IRS	U.S. Internal Revenue Service
ISA	International Society of Automation
ISO	International Organization for Standardization
ITSEC	Information Technology Security Evaluation Criteria
IUT	Implementation Under Test
JITC	Joint Interoperability Test Command
JTF-GNO	Joint Task Force – Global Networks Operation
KAT	Known Answer Test
LED	Light-Emitting Diode
MAC	Message Authentication Code
MQV	Menezes-Qu-Vanstone algorithm
NIH	U.S. National Institute of Health
NIPRNet	Non-Classified Internet Protocol Router Network
NIST	National Institute of Standards and Technology
NSTISSP	National Security Telecommunications and Information Systems Security Policy

NVLAP	National Voluntary Laboratory Accreditation Program
NVRAM	Non-Volatile Random Access Memory
OEM	Original Equipment Manufacturer
OFOM	OpenSSL FIPS Object Module
OS	Operating System
OTAR	Over-The-Air-Rekeying
PCI	Peripheral Component Interconnect
PCI	Payment Card Industry
PCI-DSS	Payment Card Industry – Data Security Standard
PII	Personally Identifiable Information
PP	Protection Profile
PRNG	Pseudo-Random Number Generator
QA	Quality Assurance
RFQ	Request for Quote
RNG	Random Number Generator
ROI	Return-on-Investment
RSA	Rivest, Shamir, Adleman
SHA	Secure Hash Algorithm
SIPRNet	Secret Internet Protocol Router Network
SOW	Statement of Work
SPA	Simple Power Analysis
SPN	Substitution Permutation Network
SSL/TLS	Secure Socket Layer/Transport Layer Security
SW	Software
T&M	Time and Materials
TDEA	Triple Data Encryption Algorithm
TOE	Target of Evaluation
TTM	Time-to-Market
URL	Universal Resource Locator
USB	Universal Serial Bus
VPN	Virtual Private Network
XOR	Exclusive OR
XOX	XOR-Encrypt-XOR
XTS	XOR-Encrypt-XOR Tweakable CodeBook mode with ciphertext stealing

REFERENCES

[**Adams**] Adams, Dawn and Erin Connor. "FIPS 140 & CC, How do they get along." September 20, 2010.
http://www.11iccc.org.tr/1%20-%20ID%2041%20Erin%20Connor%20-%20FIPS%20140%20%20CC%20%E2%80%93%20How%20do%20they%20get%20along.pdf

[**AESAVS**] Bassham, Lawrence E., III. *Advanced Encryption Standard Algorithm Validation Suite*. National Institute of Standards and Technology. November 15, 2002.
http://csrc.nist.gov/groups/STM/cavp/documents/aes/AESAVS.pdf

[**ANSI**] American National Standards Institute. *X9 Financial Industry Standards*. October 2010.
http://www.x9.org/home/

[**Army**] Department of the Army. "Letter to Industry Concerning the Approval and Acquisition of Information Assurance (IA) Tools and Products in the United States Army." December 14, 2007.

[**Army2009**] Department of the Army. "Letter to Industry Concerning the Approval and Acquisition of Information Assurance (IA) Tools and Products in the United States Army." May 21, 2009.

[**CAVL**] National Institute of Standards and Technology. "Cryptographic Algorithm Validation List." 2010.
http://csrc.nist.gov/groups/STM/cavp/validation.html

[**CAVP**] National Institute of Standards and Technology. "Cryptographic Algorithm Validation Program." 2010.
http://csrc.nist.gov/groups/STM/cavp/index.html

[**CAVP FAQ**] National Institute of Standards and Technology and Communications Security Establishment. "Frequently Asked Questions For the Cryptographic Algorithm Validation Program Concerning the Validation of Cryptographic Algorithm Implementations." August 30, 2010.

http://csrc.nist.gov/groups/STM/cavp/documents/CAVPFAQ.pdf

[CCMVS] Bassham, Lawrence E., III. *The CCM Validation System.*
National Institute of Standards and Technology. March 30, 2006.
http://csrc.nist.gov/groups/STM/cavp/documents/mac/CCMVS.pdf

[CFR] Federal Communications Commission. Electronic Code of Federal
Regulations – Title 47: Telecommunication. February 22, 2011.
http://ecfr.gpoaccess.gov/cgi/t/text/text-
idx?c=ecfr&sid=18ed3c6cb590b976a198775168c7f1e1&rgn=div5&view=te
xt&node=47:1.0.1.1.14&idno=47

[CMACVS] Keller, Sharon S. *The CMAC Validation System.* National
Institute of Standards and Technology. March 30, 2006.
http://csrc.nist.gov/groups/STM/cavp/documents/mac/CMACVS.pd
f

[CMVL] National Institute of Standards and Technology. "Module
Validation Lists." 2011.
http://csrc.nist.gov/groups/STM/cmvp/validation.html

[CMVP] National Institute of Standards and Technology.
"Cryptographic Module Validation Program." 2011.
http://csrc.nist.gov/groups/STM/cmvp/index.html

[CMVP FAQ] National Institute of Standards and Technology and
Communications Security Establishment. "Frequently Asked Questions
for the Cryptographic Module Validation Program." December 4, 2007.
http://csrc.nist.gov/groups/STM/cmvp/documents/CMVPFAQ.pdf

[CMVP MM] National Institute of Standards and Technology and
Communications Security Establishment Canada. *Cryptographic Module
Validation Program Management Manual.* April 15, 2009.
http://csrc.nist.gov/groups/STM/cmvp/documents/CMVPMM.pdf

[CSTL] National Institute of Standards and Technology. "Testing
Laboratories." February 22, 2011.
http://csrc.nist.gov/groups/STM/testing_labs/index.html

[DSAVS] Hall, Timothy A. *The FIPS 186-3 Digital Signature Algorithm Validation System.* National Institute of Standards and Technology. March 31, 2010.
http://csrc.nist.gov/groups/STM/cavp/documents/dss2/dsa2vs.pdf

[DTR] CMVP Program Staff. *Derived Test Requirements for FIPS 140-2, Security Requirements for Cryptographic Modules.* National Institute of Standards and Technology. January 4, 2011.
http://csrc.nist.gov/groups/STM/cmvp/documents/fips140-2/FIPS1402DTR.pdf

[Easter 2010] Easter, Randall J. "Cryptographic Module Validation Program." March 5, 2010.
http://biometrics.nist.gov/cs_links/ibpc2010/workII/3easter_Testing_methods_for_protecting_biometric_templates_CMVP_RJE_Presentation_03-05-2010.pdf

[ECDSAVS] Hall, Timothy A. and Sharon S. Keller. *The FIPS 186-3 Elliptic Curve Digital Signature Algorithm Validation System.* National Institute of Standards and Technology. August 30, 2010.
http://csrc.nist.gov/groups/STM/cavp/documents/dss2/ecdsa2vs.pdf

[EStats 2010] U.S. Census Bureau. "E-Stats." May 27, 2010.
http://www.census.gov/econ/estats/2008/2008reportfinal.pdf

[FCC] Electronic Code of Federal Regulations. *Title 47: Telecommunication, Part 15, Subpart B, Unintentional Radiators.* Federal Communications Commission. February 24, 2011.
http://ecfr.gpoaccess.gov/cgi/t/text/text-idx?c=ecfr&sid=1262b2b3d5460b23c87a851cedf28399&rgn=div5&view=text&node=47:1.0.1.1.14&idno=47

[FIPS 140-2] National Institute of Standards and Technology. "Standards." January 25, 2011.
http://csrc.nist.gov/groups/STM/cmvp/standards.html#02

[FIPS 140-2 A] Campbell, Jean and Randall Easter. *Annex A: Approved Security Functions for FIPS Pub 140-2, Security Requirements for Cryptographic Modules.* National Institute of Standards and Technology. January 4, 2011.
http://csrc.nist.gov/publications/fips/fips140-2/fips1402annexa.pdf

[FIPS 140-2 B] Campbell, Jean and Randall Easter. *Annex B: Approved Protection Profiles for FIPS PUB 140-2, Security Requirements for Cryptographic Modules* . National Institute of Standards and Technology. June 14, 2007.
http://csrc.nist.gov/publications/fips/fips140-2/fips1402annexb.pdf

[FIPS 140-2 C] Campbell, Jean and Randall Easter. *Annex C: Approved Random Number Generators for FIPS PUB 140-2, Security Requirements for Cryptographic Modules* . National Institute of Standards and Technology. November 24, 2010.
http://csrc.nist.gov/publications/fips/fips140-2/fips1402annexc.pdf

[FIPS 140-2 D] Campbell, Jean and Randall Easter. *Annex D: Approved Key Establishment Techniques for FIPS PUB 140-2, Security Requirements for Cryptographic Modules.* National Institute of Standards and Technology. January 4, 2011.
http://csrc.nist.gov/publications/fips/fips140-2/fips1402annexd.pdf

[FIPS 180-3] National Institute of Standards and Technology. *FIPS Publication 180-3 – Secure Hash Standard.* October 2008.
http://csrc.nist.gov/publications/fips/fips180-3/fips180-3_final.pdf

[FIPS 185] National Institute of Standards and Technology. *Escrowed Encryption Standard.* February 9, 1994.
http://csrc.nist.gov/publications/fips/fips185/fips185.txt

[FIPS 186-3] National Institute of Standards and Technology. *FIPS Publication 186-3 – Digital Signature Standard.* June 2009.
http://csrc.nist.gov/publications/fips/fips186-3/fips_186-3.pdf

[FIPS 197] National Institute of Standards and Technology. *FIPS Publication 197 – Advanced Encryption Standard.* November 26, 2001.
http://csrc.nist.gov/publications/fips/fips197/fips-197.pdf

[FIPS 198] National Institute of Standards and Technology. *FIPS Publication 198 – The Keyed-Hash Message Authentication Code (HMAC).* March 6, 2002.
http://csrc.nist.gov/publications/fips/fips198/fips-198a.pdf

[FISMA] U.S. Federal Government. Federal Information Security Management Act of 2002. 2002. http://csrc.nist.gov/drivers/documents/FISMA-final.pdf

[Gartner 2010] Gartner, Inc.. "Gartner Says Security Software Market is Poised for 11 Percent Growth in 2010." August 16, 2010. http://www.gartner.com/it/page.jsp?id=1422314

[GCMVS] Hall, Timothy A. and Sharon S. Keller. *The Galois/Counter Mode (GCM) and GMAC Validation System (GCMVS)*. National Institute of Standards and Technology. February 11, 2009. http://csrc.nist.gov/groups/STM/cavp/documents/mac/gcmvs.pdf

[HMACVS] Bassham, Lawrence E., III. *The Keyed-Hash Message Authentication Code Validation System (HMACVS)*. National Institute of Standards and Technology. December 3, 2004. http://csrc.nist.gov/groups/STM/cavp/documents/mac/HMACVS.pdf

[ICCC] International Common Criteria Conference. "International Common Criteria Conference 2010." September 2010. http://www.11iccc.org.tr/

[IG] National Institute of Standards and Technology and Communications Security Establishment. *Implementation Guidance for FIPS PUB 140-2 and the Cryptographic Module Validation Program*. December 23, 2010. http://csrc.nist.gov/groups/STM/cmvp/documents/fips140-2/FIPS1402IG.pdf

[Javelin 2009] Javelin Strategy and Research. *2009 Identity Fraud Report*. 2010. https://www.javelinstrategy.com/research/brochures/brochure-128 Referenced by: http://www.spendonlife.com/guide/2009-identity-theft-statistics

[KASVS] Keller, Sharon. S. *The Key Agreement Schemes Validation System*. National Institute of Standards and Technology. September 13, 2010. http://csrc.nist.gov/groups/STM/cavp/documents/keymgmt/KASVS.pdf

[MIP] National Institute of Standards and Technology. "Modules In Progress." February 22, 2011.
http://csrc.nist.gov/groups/STM/cmvp/inprocess.html

[MMT] National Institute of Standards and Technology. *The Multi-block Message Test (MMT) for DES and TDES.*
http://csrc.nist.gov/groups/STM/cavp/documents/des/DESMMT.pdf

[NIST RNG] Keller, Sharon S. NIST-Recommended Random Number Generator Based on ANSI X9.31 Appendix A.2.4 Using the 3-Key Triple DES and AES Algorithms. National Institute of Standards and Technology. January 31, 2005.
http://csrc.nist.gov/groups/STM/cavp/documents/rng/931rngext.pdf

[OFOM SP] Open Source Software Institute. *OpenSSL FIPS 140-2 Security Policy.* November 5, 2010.
http://csrc.nist.gov/groups/STM/cmvp/documents/140-1/140sp/140sp1051.pdf

[OFOM UG] Open Source Software Institute. *OpenSSL FIPS 140-2 User Guide.* November 21, 2009.
http://openssl.org/docs/fips/UserGuide.pdf

[OpenSSL] OpenSSL Project. "OpenSSL." March 2011.
http://openssl.org/

[OSSI] Open Source Software Institute. "FIPS Validated OpenSSL Modules." March 2011. http://www.oss-institute.org/index.php?option=com_content&view=category&layout=blog&id=140&Itemid=207

[OTAR] TIA/EIA Telecommunications Systems Bulletin, APCO Project 25. *Over-The-Air-Rekeying (OTAR) Protocol, New Technology Standards Project, Digital Radio Technical Standards, TSB102.AACA.* Telecommunications Industry Association. January, 1996.

[Rijndael] Daemen, Joan and Vincent Rijmen. *AES Proposal: Rijndael.* September 3, 1999. http://csrc.nist.gov/archive/aes/rijndael/Rijndael-ammended.pdf

[RNGVS] Bassham, Lawrence E., III. *The Random Number Generator Validation System (RNGVS)*. National Institute of Standards and Technology. January 31, 2005.
http://csrc.nist.gov/groups/STM/cavp/documents/rng/RNGVS.pdf

[RSA DES] RSA Corporation. "RSA Code-Breaking Contest Again Won by Distributed.Net and Electronic Frontier Foundation (EFF)." January 19, 1999.
http://www.rsa.com/press_release.aspx?id=462

[RSAVS] Keller, Sharon. S. *The RSA Validation System*. National Institute of Standards and Technology. November 4, 2004.
http://csrc.nist.gov/groups/STM/cavp/documents/dss/RSAVS.pdf

[SHAVS] Bassham, Lawrence E., III. *The Secure Hash Algorithm Validation System (SHAVS)*. National Institute of Standards and Technology. July 22, 2004.
http://csrc.nist.gov/groups/STM/cavp/documents/shs/SHAVS.pdf

[Skipjack] Skipjack and KEA Algorithm Specifications. May 29, 1998.
http://csrc.nist.gov/groups/STM/cavp/documents/skipjack/skipjack.pdf

[SP 800-17] Keller, Sharon and Miles Smid. *Modes of Operation Validation System (MOVS): Requirements and Procedures*. National Institute of Standards and Technology. February 1998.
http://csrc.nist.gov/publications/nistpubs/800-17/800-17.pdf

[SP 800-20] Keller, Sharon. *Modes of Operation Validation System for the Triple Data Encryption Algorithm (TMOVS): Requirements and Procedures*. National Institute of Standards and Technology. April 2000.
http://csrc.nist.gov/publications/nistpubs/800-20/800-20.pdf

[SP 800-38A] Dworkin, Morris. *Recommendations for Block Cipher Modes of Operation: Methods and Techniques*. National Institute of Standards and Technology. December 2001.
http://csrc.nist.gov/publications/nistpubs/800-38a/sp800-38a.pdf

[SP 800-38B] Dworkin, Morris. *Recommendation for Block Cipher Modes of Operation: The CMAC Mode of Authentication*. National Institute of Standards and Technology. May 2005. http://csrc.nist.gov/publications/nistpubs/800-38B/SP_800-38B.pdf

[SP 800-38C] Dworkin, Morris. Recommendation for Block Cipher Modes of Operation: The CCM Mode for Authentication and Confidentiality. National Institute of Standards and Technology. May 2004. http://csrc.nist.gov/publications/nistpubs/800-38C/SP800-38C.pdf

[SP 800-38D] Dworkin, Morris. *Recommendation for Block Cipher Modes of Operation: Galois/Counter Mode (GCM) and GMAC*. National Institute of Standards and Technology. November 2007. http://csrc.nist.gov/publications/nistpubs/800-38D/SP-800-38D.pdf

[SP 800-38E] Dworkin, Morris. Recommendation for Block Cipher Modes of Operation: The XTS-AES Mode of Confidentiality on Storage Devices. National Institute of Standards and Technology. January 2010. http://csrc.nist.gov/publications/nistpubs/800-38E/nist-sp-800-38E.pdf

[SP 800-56A] Barker, Elaine and others. *Recommendation for Pair-Wise Key Establishment Schemes Using Discrete Logorithm Cryptography*. National Institute of Standards and Technology. March 2007. http://csrc.nist.gov/publications/nistpubs/800-56A/SP800-56A_Revision1_Mar08-2007.pdf

[SP 800-56B] Barker, Elaine and others. *Recommendation for Pair-Wise Key Establishment Schemes Using Integer Factorization Cryptography*. National Institute of Standards and Technology. August 2009. http://csrc.nist.gov/publications/nistpubs/800-56B/sp800-56B.pdf

[SP 800-57] Barker, Elaine and others. *Recommendation for Key Management – Part 1: General*. National Institute of Standards and Technology. March 2007. http://csrc.nist.gov/publications/nistpubs/800-57/sp800-57-Part1-revised2_Mar08-2007.pdf

[SP 800-90] Barker, Elaine and John Kelsey. *Recommendation for Random Number Generation Using Deterministic Random Bit Generators.* National Institute of Standards and Technology. March 2007. http://csrc.nist.gov/publications/nistpubs/800-90/SP800-90revised_March2007.pdf

[SP 800-131A] Barker, Elaine and Allen Roginsky. *Transitions: Recommendation for the Transitioning of Cryptographic Algorithms and Key Lengths.* National Institute of Standards and Technology. January 2011. http://csrc.nist.gov/publications/nistpubs/800-131A/sp800-131A.pdf

[TDEA] Barker, William. *Recommendation for the Triple Data Encryption Algorithm (TDEA) Block Cipher.* National Institute of Standards and Technology. Version 1.1. May 2004. http://csrc.nist.gov/publications/nistpubs/800-67/SP800-67.pdf

[XTSVS] Keller, Sharon S. and Timothy A. Hall. *The XTS-AES Validation System.* National Institute of Standards and Technology. August 30, 2010 http://csrc.nist.gov/groups/STM/cavp/documents/aes/XTSVS.pdf

INDEX

A

accreditation, 68, 76, 195, 205
accredited, 26, 56, 68, 74, 76, 79, 80, 85, 88, 91, 169, 173, 188, 195, 198
acquisition, 159
add-ons, 131
Adleman, 60, 152, 205
Advanced Encryption Standard, 25, 34, 58, 59, 62, 152, 203
agency, 68
agent, 26, 32
agreement, 64, 186
alternative, 59, 107, 151, 201
ANSI, 59, 63, 64, 65, 203
anti-spyware, 137
anti-virus, 33, 34, 137, 139
application programmatic interfaces, 143, 151
application-specific integrated circuits, 129
approval, 159, 162, 183
architecture, 195
arguments, 163
ASCII, 41
assertions, 37, 38, 39, 177, 178
assessments, 81, 197

assurance, 9, 11, 13, 26, 38, 39, 67, 68, 72, 80, 88, 115, 116, 123, 124, 125, 129, 138, 141, 174, 175, 195, 197, 198
attackers, 25, 29, 34, 42, 112, 130, 179
attempts, 100, 103, 180
attributes, 178, 179
augments, 74, 189
authenticate, 98, 133
authorized, 35, 41, 46, 48, 98, 99, 113, 115, 119, 121, 132, 133
availability, 29, 159, 179, 191

B

bandwidth, 35, 135, 147
benchmark, 94
benefits, 38, 163
binary, 41, 153
biometrics, 49
bits, 34, 41, 49, 58, 62, 63, 197
black-box, 55
blocks, 46, 58, 60
breaches, 29, 32, 37
budget, 26, 165, 166, 191
business-to-business, 29, 31
business-to-customer, 31

expenses, 26, 82, 83, 84, 163

F

factor, 49, 83, 86, 88, 94
Federal Communications
 Commission, 74, 112, 139, 204
fees, 79, 87, 163, 191
Feistel, 59
Finite State Model, 72, 73, 74, 77,
 81, 84, 92, 93, 95, 101, 121, 189,
 190, 198, 204
FIPS 140 compliant, 147, 174,
 175
FIPS-approved, 55, 74
firewalls, 33, 34, 129, 137
firmware, 69, 71, 74, 92, 93, 94,
 95, 96, 113, 114, 119, 122, 123,
 125, 129, 132, 138, 149, 153,
 160, 176, 177, 178, 179, 185,
 187, 196
FISMA, 37, 134, 161, 204
fixed-length, 46, 58
fixed-price, 83, 84, 191, 198, 201
flaws, 39, 51, 201
fraud, 30
functional, 56, 57, 141, 151, 175,
 176, 199
functionality, 55, 67, 68, 73, 75,
 76, 79, 80, 149, 151, 159, 179,
 180

G

Galois/Counter, 61, 62, 204
general-purpose, 59, 71, 108,
 109, 123, 133, 139, 144
generators, 49, 60, 63, 109
goal, 86, 134, 187, 191

H

hacker, 34
hardware, 28, 67, 71, 92, 94, 95,
 96, 106, 116, 119, 120, 122, 125,
 129, 130, 131, 132, 133, 134,
 135, 138, 139, 140, 144, 146,
 149, 152, 153, 159, 160, 166,
 176, 177, 178, 179, 180, 187,
 196, 200
hash, 45, 46, 47, 60, 63, 96, 198
hexadecimal, 41
host, 71, 144
hybrid, 49, 69, 153

I

identification, 30, 89, 118
identity theft, 29, 30, 37
identity-based, 92, 95, 118
implementation under test, 72,
 74, 77, 198
implementations, 55, 56, 57, 68,
 116, 123
independent, 26, 38, 39, 55, 68,
 69, 76, 79, 80, 84, 129, 173, 195,
 198
initialization, 99, 125, 149, 153
installation, 34, 92, 116, 125, 141,
 173, 187
integrated circuit, 71, 105, 122
internationally-recognized, 187,
 195
interpretation, 70
interval, 155
intrusion detection systems, 33,
 34
invalidate, 148, 173
investment, 79, 134, 163, 170,
 191
invoices, 31, 32

Z

Made in the USA
San Bernardino, CA
09 July 2014